Engineering Aspects of Supervisory Management

Studies in Supervisory Management

SERIES EDITOR: JOHN MUNRO FRASER

Engineering Aspects of Supervisory Management

K. A. NORTON, B.Sc AMIProdE AMBIM
Lecturer in Management Studies
Solihull Technical College

JOHN MUNRO FRASER MA
Reader in the Department of
Industrial Administration
University of Aston in Birmingham

NELSON

THOMAS NELSON AND SONS LTD
36 Park Street London W1
P.O. Box 2187 Accra
P.O. Box 336 Apapa Lagos
P.O. Box 25012 Nairobi
P.O. Box 21149 Dar es Salaam
77 Coffee Street San Fernando Trinidad

THOMAS NELSON (AUSTRALIA) LTD
597 Little Collins Street Melbourne C1

THOMAS NELSON AND SONS (SOUTH AFRICA)
(PROPRIETARY) LTD
51 Commissioner Street Johannesburg

THOMAS NELSON AND SONS (CANADA) LTD
81 Curlew Drive Don Mills Ontario

THOMAS NELSON AND SONS
Copewood and Davis Streets Camden New Jersey 08103

First published in Great Britain 1968

© K. A. Norton and John Munro Fraser 1968

17 175143 4

Made and Printed in Great Britain by
Thomas Nelson (Printers) Ltd, London and Edinburgh

Preface

Experience in the jobs he was supervising, some ability to organize day-to-day working, and a certain ruthlessness in dealing with the people under his charge—in the year 1900, this would have equipped a man quite adequately for the job of a foreman. Management methods in those days were simple and straightforward, for the practitioners of work study, quality control, production planning and the like, had not yet begun to make their influence felt. Since that date, however, there have been developments in the technique of management, and there are now few organisations where one or other of these functions is not represented by a specialist department.

Such departments provide an essential service to the supervisory manager. But it is the use he makes of these services which determines how far they actually contribute towards efficient working. And he will only make effective use of them if he has a general understanding of their purpose and methods. This book is intended to help towards such an understanding. It does not claim to equip the reader to practise value analysis, production control or job evaluation. Any one of these would require a detailed text to itself. It aims simply to describe these specializations as they affect the job of the supervisory manager, and to enable him to collaborate intelligently with the representatives he may encounter in day-to-day working. The general outline has been adapted to the Technical Aspects syllabus of the National Examinations Board for Supervisory Studies. The authors hope that it will be found useful by students seeking this qualification, the importance of which is becoming increasingly recognized in modern industry.

K.A.N.

J.M.F.

Contents

7   Quality Control or Inspection   91
Value Analysis—Summary

8   Production Planning and Control   104
The Study of a Production Problem—Putting the Plan into
Action—The Production Control System—Summary

9   Records and Statistics   120
The Collection of Data—Presentation of Statistical Data—
Sampling—Graphs—The Z-Chart—Histograms or Block
Frequency Diagrams—Variance—Quality Control Charts—
Records for the Supervisory Manager—Management by
Objectives—Summary

Further Reading   142

Index   143

CHAPTER 1 | Introduction

If we took a chap from a country district and put him in the middle of a modern engineering works, he'd find it a pretty bewildering place. There would be machinery all around him, cutting or stamping or drilling. There would be moving conveyor lines carrying work from one process to the next. There would be people operating machines, driving fork-lift trucks, noting figures on clip-boards, or just standing around looking worried. He wouldn't have a clue about what was going on.

Even if he asked someone to tell him what was happening he mightn't be any better off. He would probably get a stream of gibberish about half-thou tolerances, standard minutes, job evaluations, rates of overhead recovery—all in terms he'd never heard before and couldn't guess the meaning of. Each factory has its own ʼanguage, its own ideas, and its own way of working. Anyone who tries to lay down the law about British industry very soon finds himself talking nonsense.

But if we are going to understand what is going on—and more important, if we are going to exercise any control—we must try to work out some general principles. We must arrive at some ideas by which we can interpret any process in any factory; and the simpler these ideas, the more useful they will be. For example, in any factory there will be raw material coming in at one end, and finished products going out at the other. The raw material will cost money—so much a ton, so much a yard, or so much a piece. The finished products will be sold for money also—more money than was paid for the raw material. And the difference between the two prices will be the amount of money available to pay all the expenses of the factory. This is one of the simplest possible ideas, but it is of universal application in manufacturing industry.

You may feel, of course, that it is too simple to be of much use to anyone. But if you stop for a moment and think of the problems faced by a Board of Directors at the end of the financial year, you will realize how fundamental this idea is. Unless there is enough margin between these two sums of money, the directors will have a hard time persuading the shareholders to let them keep their jobs. And even though they may get away with it this year, they'll have to put up a better show at the next annual general meeting.

Productive Efficiency and who benefits from it

In this book we shall discuss the general ideas that help to explain what goes on in an engineering works. They may not apply in detail in any one factory; every factory, however, will illustrate how they work in practice. We shall see also how these ideas or principles could be applied to make any factory more efficient.

This word 'efficiency' crops up in most discussions about industrial management. But what exactly do we mean by it? Can we recognize efficiency when we see it? Can we say that one factory is more efficient than another? Most important of all, can we measure efficiency?

We have here another idea of general application, and we might spend a moment getting it clear. The best measure of efficiency is cost. And we have made a factory more efficient when we have cut down any aspect of its costs, measured in money terms. If we have shortened the time it takes to carry out a task, we have saved money in direct wages. If we have produced less scrap, we have saved money in less wasted material. If we have used less room, we have saved money in expensive floor space. If we have cut down waiting time, we have saved money in less work-in-progress lying around. And if we have kept machines running nearer their full capacity, we have saved money in a better rate of overhead recovery. When we think of efficiency, therefore, we should think in terms of pounds, shillings, and pence. And we should be aiming at increasing the margin between the cost of the material and what the customer pays for the finished product.

But, you may ask, who benefits from this increased efficiency? Does the money saved go straight into the pockets of the shareholders? If that's what happens, there's not much in it for you, is there? So why should you bother? This is quite a reasonable point of view, and it raises a question we should clear up before we go on. In any situation which involves people, the question 'What's in it for me?' should never be lost sight of.

The result of increased efficiency is more money in the kitty, as we have said. But there are several groups of people who want to get their hands on this money. Each of these groups has a perfect right to make its demand. And in a fully employed, competitive society like present-day Britain, each has a means of backing up its claim. Customers want better value in lower prices or higher quality. And if they don't get it, they'll take their business elsewhere. Employees want higher wages and salaries. They can bargain collectively through trade unions or they can shop around individually for better jobs if they're not satisfied. Suppliers want the best price they can get for their raw material. And if there's a shortage, they'll be quick to take advantage of it. The directors want more to plough back in new plant and equipment. If they don't get it, the factory will soon be out of date. The shareholders want higher dividends and they want to see the value of their shares going up on the Stock Exchange. If this doesn't happen, they'll be ready to accept a take-over bid. The Government wants more in taxes. And if it doesn't get its rake-off, we won't have our Health Service, our new motorways, or our Welfare State. All these groups are competing for their share in the takings. And in a free enterprise society, each one can bring its own kind of pressure to bear.

Any industrial enterprise must be able to stand up to competition if it is to survive. And in the present-day world there is competition for markets, for supplies, for capital, for labour, and for everything else on which the company's existence depends. This competition must be met from the resources available to it. In simple terms, these resources are the money it makes from the difference between cost and selling price. If this is insufficient to meet all these competing demands, the company will soon be out of business. No one should be worried, therefore, about increased efficiency resulting in more money for the company. He'll get his share sooner or later, one way or the other. The danger is when the company begins to run short. Then he should really begin to worry, for then his job may disappear. And if other companies are in the same state, there won't be any other jobs. And if the Government is short of money too, his unemployment benefit may be in danger as well. This is the state we were in during the nineteen-twenties and 'thirties. And no one wants to see those days back again.

The General Ideas behind Productive Industry

We are going to look at a number of ideas or general principles which apply to any manufacturing company. Before we get down to detail, it might be useful to run through them quickly. For each one will have its effect on how the business is run. Each one will also affect the others, so that together they will determine the company's way of working.

(1) First of all there will be a *Market Factor*. It is the customer who really decides what is going to be produced, so we should be finding out as much about him as we can. If there are only a few possible customers, and each one wants something special to suit his own

particular needs, this will determine the whole production process. It will have to be on a 'one-off' basis, with each product made to the customer's specification. If, however, there are lots of customers, their requirements will probably all have something in common. Products can then be more or less standardized and made in batches, or perhaps on a 'flow' basis. This will demand a different kind of production process, with different types of plant and different kinds of job. It will also affect the cost, for there are economies in large-scale production. When we look at any manufacturing enterprise, therefore, we should always start by considering this market factor.

(2) Next there will be a *Design Factor*. If the market consists of a few customers, each with his own special requirements, products must be designed to suit these. This means that each order will be a 'special' and the designer must devote all his attention to what the customer wants. But if there are plenty of customers, the designer must think about the common elements in the products they require. And he must try to design something that will meet as many of these as he can. This is where some standardization becomes possible— and also where the designer must pay more attention to the production process. If he can design something which is easy to produce in quantity, he will be making a faster production flow through the factory possible. Of course, if he can design a completely standard article which satisfies all customers, then the production process itself can be standardized. The designer thus stands between the market and the production process. And his job is to bring the two together as closely as possible.

(3) Following on from these will be a *Plant and Equipment Factor*. If the designer has to produce a series of 'specials', then the machinery must be capable of adapting to each job in turn. This will involve different settings for a series of one-off jobs and individual control of each machine. If, however, the designer has managed to standardize the product, longer runs will become possible. Machines can then be simplified to produce these standard parts, and there will be less need for individual setting. If this process of standardization can be pushed still further, continuous process machinery will become practicable. Special equipment can then be designed so that the product can be fed from one to the next. This is the process of 'automation' which grows out of the market and the design factors. Automated equipment is much more complex and expensive than what is required for one-off production. But it can deal with a much greater flow of production at a much lower cost.

(4) We now come to a *Personnel Factor*, which is concerned with

the kind of people we need to do the jobs. This again will depend on what we have discussed above, for one-off production will demand highly skilled and responsible operators. Each must be capable of doing a range of jobs and maintaining a high standard of quality. Each must be able to make his own decisions on day-to-day matters. This applies even more to his supervisor who must also have skill and experience in the trade. When we move to flow production, however, the nature of the job will change. Working on standard parts needs less skill, for the same task has simply to be done over and over again. A different type of supervisor will also be required, one who can understand the process as a whole and collaborate with the specialist departments which now become more important. If flow production gives way to automation, we need a different type of operator again. He must now be a technician, trained in the very complex equipment and capable of controlling it, usually by electronic means. Each of these different types of job must be studied and analysed to make sure that the right method is determined, the right type of man trained for it, and the right means of control devised, to ensure that he is working effectively.

(5) *A Production Control Factor* must now be considered. This is aimed at ensuring that the flow of work is kept moving and that the operators and equipment are fully employed. It is concerned with the provision of material at the beginning of the process; with the programming of production so that each section of the plant is kept fully occupied; and with the smooth movement of partially finished products from one process to the next. In one-off production this factor is very much in the hands of the man in charge on the shop floor, for long-term detailed planning is difficult. With flow production, however, production control becomes a specialist function. Longer-term planning not only becomes possible; it becomes essential if the advantages of this type of production are to be realized. A production programme for the whole factory can be laid out in advance, and broken down for each section. The supply of material can be planned so that no shortages hold up the production process. Each section programme should provide that the partially finished products flow from one section to the next and keep each occupied to full capacity.

(6) *A Quality Control or Inspection Factor.* If products are to be sold they must conform to a specification, and checks must be carried out to ensure that they do so. With one-off production this will involve individual inspection at convenient stages, and will usually be carried out by the skilled operator and the man immediately in

Market Factor	Design Factor	Plant and Equipment Factor
Few customers, each requiring a special product and prepared to wait for it to be made at the appropriate price.	Each product specially designed to meet customer's own requirements.	Machines capable of adapting to a range of products, usually involving individual setting and operation.
More customers wanting products with common elements, expecting quick delivery and cheaper prices.	Standardization and rationalization of parts and products, designed with production methods in mind.	Machinery capable of producing long runs of standard parts, usually requiring simpler setting and adjustment, with the use of jigs or fixtures.
A mass market wanting immediate delivery of large quantities of the same product at very cheap prices.	Standard products designed for production in quantity by automated equipment.	Highly complex automated equipment working on continuous process.

FIG. 1. *Factors which affect the production process*

Personnel Factor	Production Control Factor	Quality Control or Inspection Factor	Cost Factor
Highly skilled operators capable of a range of jobs, day-to-day decisions and high quality.	Material ordered as required for individual jobs. Planning carried out by person immediately in charge.	Each job inspected according to individual standards. Considerable responsibility on man immediately in charge.	Each job estimated individually. Considerable responsibility on man in charge to keep direct labour and materials within estimate.
Semi-skilled operators carrying out standardized tasks on a repetitive basis, with little responsibility for decisions.	Orders placed in advance for material. Work planned ahead by specialists to provide for long runs.	Regular check at key points to pre-determined standards by specially trained inspectors.	Estimates based on long runs in considerable detail. Reponsibility on man in charge to achieve planned cost targets.
Technician-level operators trained to understand and control complex equipment, taking decisions of long-term importance.	Regular and continuous flow of material in quantity. Production planned on long-term to keep expensive equipment running to capacity.	Quantity-control built into equipment, requiring continuous supervision by operator.	Estimates based on maximum use of equipment in continuous production. Responsibility on man in charge to keep equipment running.

charge. A final inspection against the customer's requirements may be made by a specialist or even by the customer's representative. With standard products on flow production, a series of regular checks can be planned to predetermined standards. These can be made by inspectors specially trained beforehand. Responsibility for carrying out these checks may then be removed from the supervisor, though it will still be his task to ensure that defects are put right and quality maintained. With automation, quality control can usually be built into the equipment itself.

(7) *A Cost Factor* runs through every stage of the process. This begins with an estimate of the materials required and with their prices. Next comes an estimate of the man-hours, with the various wage rates involved. A further sum must be added for indirect charges, overheads, and the like. Taken together, these will give an idea of the total cost of the product. In one-off production this is likely to include a margin of error, as these estimates must cover a number of contingencies. With flow production they should be more accurate, as past experience can provide more adequate information. There is, however, another aspect to this factor which can be even more important. This is the checking up to see that the cost of the product has in fact been kept within the estimate. It is by this cost-control factor that the efficiency of the factory is kept under review. As we said above, money provides a very useful measure, for every aspect of a factory's working can be expressed in money terms. Thus if wages, materials, plant utilization, overhead recovery, and the like are all kept within the estimates, the company has everything under control.

Some of these factors will be beyond the scope of the supervisory manager. He will usually have little to do with investigating the market or with the design of the product. He will not be involved in the purchase of new plant, nor will he be concerned with estimating cost. His work is more down-to-earth, making sure that day-to-day production is kept going. But all these factors will affect his job, and he will do it better if he has some idea of them. He might, in fact, be asked for advice on one or other of them. If, for example, the Market Factor makes only one-off production possible, he should understand the reasons. And he should be able to talk sense if there is any discussion about trying to standardize products in the hope of extending the market. This is the background which determines the kind of job he has to do. And the more he appreciates its limitations, the more insight he will have into his own job.

The job of the supervisor has been described as the management of men, machines, material, methods, and money. But he is doing all this within a framework of organization determined by outside factors—markets and design. How he manages these five 'M's' will depend on this framework. And the table in Fig. 1 shows how this framework relates to his job.

The Job of the Supervisor

How all these factors affect the supervisory manager's job should now be clear. If he is in charge of a one-off section, he will have wide responsibility for its day-to-day working. He will allocate tasks to the skilled operators under his charge, advise them on methods, and check the quality of their work. If they run into any difficulty, he will provide the answer. He will ensure that the material required is there when it is wanted and that the best use is made of the machines. The costs of the section will be very much in his hands, for only he can ensure that labour and material are being used to the best advantage. He will be responsible for many day-to-day decisions on the various factors we have been discussing. He will, in fact, be running the section very much on his own and being judged on its results.

The supervisory manager in charge of a flow production section, however, has a rather different job. A great deal of the planning will be taken over by functional specialists, and his responsibility will now be to put the plans into action. The jobs of the operators will have been laid out by the production engineer and most of the skill and judgment will have been work-studied out of them. Each operator's job will have been planned at a particular stage in the production process and the standards of quality will have been laid down. The supervisor's responsibility will now be to ensure that these jobs are being carried out to the standard required in the planned time. The production programme will also have been planned by a specialist along with a flow of the necessary material. The supervisor's responsibility will be to ensure that this programme is carried out and that there are no interruptions to the process. If he foresees the possibility of this he must get hold of the responsible specialist and put him into action in time to prevent the flow breaking down. Supervising a flow production section is no longer a matter of taking charge of a series of individual skilled jobs. It is rather the co-ordination of a series of factors to achieve a result which has been planned in advance by someone else.

When the production process moves to automation, the supervisory manager's job changes again. Not only has the objective been planned in advance; now the method of achieving it has been worked out in detail also. Day-to-day running looks after itself and small-scale variations are taken care of by the equipment. So long as this is running according to plan, neither the operators nor the supervisor have very much to do, apart from technical control of the process. But in view of the fact that even a minor breakdown can have the most serious consequences, it is now their job to see that there is no possible risk of such a breakdown. This will involve a detailed understanding of the technology both of the equipment and of the materials.

The supervisory manager will always be the man in charge of the working section. In the last resort, its working efficiency will depend on him. As the organization develops, however, there will be more functional specialists concerned with different aspects of its working. Quality controllers will devise more advanced methods of checking standards. Production engineers will study layouts to improve the flow of work-in-progress. Work study men will be concerned with methods on individual operations. Production controllers will deal with machine-loadings and progress through the shops. All of these, and possibly others also, will make their contribution to efficient working.

These contributions, however, will always be indirect. For it is not the methods the specialists devise that make the real difference. It is the application of these methods in day-to-day working. And the effectiveness of this application depends on the supervisory manager. This is why he must understand what the specialists are trying to do. In the following chapters we shall present the general ideas which underlie the work of these functional specialists. Our account will necessarily be simple, partly because our space is limited. This, however, is not a book for the specialist. He will want a deeper and more detailed treatment of each subject. Rather, we are trying to explain these developments as they affect the job of the supervisory manager—to give a factory-floor view of them. For it is on the factory floor that productive work is done. And it is there that the efficiency of the operations is determined.

SUMMARY

1 *What do we mean by 'efficiency'?*

This is one of the general ideas we must use to understand what is going on in industry. The best measure of efficiency is cost, wage cost, material cost, floor space, overheads, and so on. Any increase in efficiency improves the margin between what is paid out in an organization and the revenue received from sales.

2 *Who benefits from increased efficiency?*

Everyone connected with an organization has a claim on its trading margin: employees, customers, suppliers, shareholders, the Government. Each has a means of backing up its claim. Unless the organization is constantly increasing its margin, these claims will remain unsatisfied and the organization will suffer.

3 *What factors are involved in production industry?*

(a) *A Market Factor* depending on the number of customers and their requirements.

(b) *A Design Factor* concerned with translating these requirements into products.

(c) *A Plant and Equipment Factor* providing the machinery to make these products.

(d) *A Personnel Factor* concerned with the individuals who work on the jobs.

(e) *A Production Control Factor* aiming at maintaining a fast and continuous flow of raw material into finished products.

(f) *A Quality Control or Inspection Factor* to ensure that products are up to specification.

(g) *A Cost Factor* concerned with estimating the cost of products and ensuring that actual costs are within these estimates.

4 *What different types of production are there?*

(a) *One-off or Jobbing Production*, where items are designed specially to customers' requirements and made in a jobbing shop by skilled operators.

(b) *Large-batch or Flow Production*, where products have been standardized and are made in quantity by semi-skilled operators working on standardized tasks.

(c) *Automated Production*, where both the products and the method of production have been standardized so that the whole process is mechanized.

The divisions between these are not always clear-cut. There are borderline cases where flow production shades into automation.

5 *How do these different methods of production affect the job of the supervisory manager?*

In a jobbing shop he will be very much in control of the day-to-day working and will make his own decisions on a wide range of matters. In flow production more of the planning will have been carried out by functional specialists. His task will be to see that the plans of these specialists are put into action effectively on the floor of the shop. This means that he must know more about what the specialists are trying to do, so that he can collaborate intelligently with them.

CHAPTER 2 | The Factory and its Layout

Before we can start production, we must have a factory to work in. And we want this factory to be as convenient as possible. The trouble is, however, that there are a lot of different aspects to consider.

Problems of the Site
The site, for example. Would it be more convenient to have the factory in a town or in the country? In a town it will be easier to get labour, and there will be rail and road transport on hand. But it will cost more, for land is expensive in towns and it is getting scarcer. Also, if we want to build an extension later on, we shall come up against planning restrictions. We might be prevented from extending in the town, and made to go somewhere else to provide employment in a Development Area. In the country, of course, land is likely to be cheaper and more easily available. But we could end up miles from anywhere. We might have difficulty in getting labour and our transport costs would be a good deal higher.

There is no such thing as the ideal site. Wherever we build a factory we shall have to balance advantages and disadvantages. Each factory is, therefore, a sort of compromise between the two. But this compromise has got to be lived with and we can look at it in two different ways. Either we can stress the advantages and use our ingenuity to overcome the disadvantages. Or we can keep shedding tears about how the disadvantages make it impossible to get anything done, while closing our eyes to the advantages. A great deal depends on which attitude we take.

Much the same goes for the building. A single-storey structure can make use of natural lighting; it makes internal transport easier; the foundations can be planned to stand up to the weight of heavy machinery; and it doesn't cost so much to erect. It takes up a lot of ground, however, and where this is expensive it may be better to put up a multi-storey structure. This will probably cost less per square foot of floor space, but it will involve lifts and stairways which will complicate the internal transport problems. It will also require more careful provision for fire escapes, means of access, and so on. On the other hand, it will be easier to heat and ventilate, though it will need more artificial lighting. Here again a compromise will be necessary, dictated by outside conditions. And here again the

13

supervisory manager will find himself in a building which is not ideal, but which he must make the best of.

In the planning of a new factory, these things must be studied and the best compromise worked out. The supervisory manager, however, is not likely to find himself involved in planning such a project, though it could happen when a company is considering an extension or a move. He might then be asked for his opinion. Normally, however, he will be working in an existing building and making the best of what is available. Once again, he's working within a framework laid down by factors outside his control. The more he understands about this framework, the better he'll be placed to know what's possible and what isn't. Let us think, therefore, about some of the factors involved in the planning of a building.

Factory Layout

First of all there are the demands of the production process. If this is based on large pieces of fixed equipment or the continuous flow of heavy material, the layout will practically decide itself. We shall, in fact, have to build the factory around the production process. A final assembly line in a motor-car factory, for example, demands a long shop with no intervening walls or obstacles. A process which depends on overhead cranes demands solid, high walls and large clear spaces. Where factors like these are important, the overall layout will remain the same so long as the process continues. Where the plant and equipment is lighter, it can be moved around more easily. Thus, changes in the layout can be made to suit new products and new production methods.

It would be a good idea for the supervisory manager to stand back for a moment and think about his own section. What comes in at one end? What goes out at the other? And what happens in between? In some cases, as with a large rolling mill, the process will determine the layout and any changes will involve heavy capital expenditure. So far as the supervisory manager is concerned, therefore, it will remain fixed for the next few years. But in other cases it won't be so difficult to move things around. He should then consider whether the layout is as convenient as it might be: whether it provides for an easy flow of production through the section; whether there is a logical sequence of operations; and whether the internal transport is being used effectively. One point worth considering is whether the work flows straight through or whether it goes backwards and forwards in its progress.

Not all the floor space, of course, will be taken up by plant and equipment. Gangways will be required to allow for movement through the factory. Some space will be needed for the temporary storage of material and work-in-progress. The operators themselves will need room to work in. And the supervisor will need an office, or at least a screened-off desk, where he can get a little peace and quiet. Here again, a compromise is necessary. Floor space costs money, and on an expensive town site it can cost quite a lot of money. To run a factory efficiently, therefore, we should be making maximum use of every square foot. One way to do this is to use the 'up' space, storing articles on top of each other where possible. On the other hand, if the place is so cluttered up that we can't move around without bumping into things, there will be delays and dangers. Safety must always be a first consideration. Thus, the problem is to make the best possible use of the floor space available, while at the same time providing for gangways, enough room for people to move around safely, and adequate space for work-in-progress.

A further problem will be internal transport. Products have to move from one machine to the next, and they should do so with as little delay as possible. Anything standing still is costing money, and the sooner it moves on, the more efficiently we are working. Always remember that when anything is put down it has to be picked up again. In a jobbing factory, this will be a matter of constant small decisions, and where the products are heavy or bulky, the means of transport will probably be overhead cranes or fork-lift trucks. The supervisory manager will thus have to be on watch to see that things get shifted as soon as possible. With larger quantities, a more regular movement of products should be aimed at. The ideal is the moving conveyor where production flows steadily through the factory from one operation to the next. Here again, the cost factor crops up, for this kind of equipment is expensive. And the expense will only be justified if constant use be made of it to full capacity. It may be better and cheaper, therefore, to plan for a regular round by the labourer with his bin or trolley, to keep things moving in a steady flow.

Once more, it would be a good idea for the supervisor to stand back for a moment and think about his own section. How is the movement of products arranged at the moment? Of course, it is always possible that this has never been considered as a problem. If the products are small bits of assembly, then people carry them around as they are needed, or go and get some when they run short. But this can waste a lot of time, either by people walking about unnecessarily or by running short of material. Output per operator is lower than it might be. It would be much better if someone thought of transport as a service—a service necessary to the factory as a whole. This transport service can then be planned to integrate the movement of products within the individual section into the overall flow of production.

This, of course, raises another aspect of factory layout. There are many services which must be provided, some which will be needed by every section, others more specialized. Most sections will need some form of motive power, for example, and nowadays this is normally provided by the electric motor. The forests of belts and shafting that used to be seen in many factories have disappeared, and individual power units have taken their place. These motors require current, which also provides the lighting, so there must be a wiring system to bring this where it is needed. The power supply must be adequate to the loads expected at every point, for we can't have fuses blowing all over the place. Some processes need a supply of compressed air; others call for a flow of water for cooling or the carrying away of waste matter; others again need stepped-up ventilation to get rid of fumes or gases, and so on. Once again, it will be interesting for the supervisor to stand back and think about the central services that must be laid on for this section. He might be able to give useful advice, if any changes are being considered.

Production Flow

The method of production will affect the means of planning and control. In a jobbing shop, the problem will be to keep track of a number of different products, each being made to a special design. With automation, the problem will be to keep expensive plant in continuous operation. There are, however, two basic aims that should always be kept in mind in production planning. These are:

(1) To achieve maximum utilization of plant and personnel.
(2) To keep raw material stocks and work-in-progress at the lowest safe level.

To some extent these are in conflict with each other.

The cost factor plays a very large part in both of these aims, and this is why they must be clearly understood by the supervisory manager. Plant and equipment cost money, and we can only recover their cost if we get production out of them. Personnel have to be paid wages or salaries, and we can't hand out money for people to stand around doing nothing. Our first aim, therefore, is to make sure that machines are working as near capacity as is practicable during the hours the factory is open. And also that our personnel are fully occupied on truly productive work while they are in the place. If you think this sounds like slave-driving, then you shouldn't be a supervisory manager. An industrial company is an economic enterprise and its survival depends on the margin between its sales revenue and its costs. Fair working conditions and good human relations on the job have their place, and they make an important contribution to efficient working. But an industrial company has to justify its existence in economic terms. And it will never do this unless it makes adequate use of its resources in productive work.

Raw materials and work-in-progress cost money too. And this money usually has to be borrowed, which means that interest has to be paid on it. Thus, if the stores are piled with slow-moving stocks of raw material and the factory littered with piles of half-finished products, we have too much money tied up in the process. We want to cut our raw material stocks to the minimum, therefore, though this minimum will depend on a number of factors. We mustn't run the risk of holding up production through shortage of material, for this would mean plant and personnel standing idle. We must have a margin of safety, which will depend on delivery dates, economic quantities, and so on. Similarly, with work-in-progress. We want this kept continuously on the move, but again we must have a margin of safety. We can't risk a hold-up in one section bringing the whole factory to a standstill.

Factors like these must be borne in mind as we plan to achieve these two main aims. In planning the layout of a factory or a section, we are trying to ensure a flow of work which will be as fast as possible. This means that we must foresee any points where work-in-progress could be held up through faulty placing of machinery or equipment. Any decision about the layout will be put to the test when production actually begins. Are there any ways in which we can foresee the problems which will be presented? Are there any means by which we can try things out, before we commit ourselves to the expense of installing the plant or building the factory?

Planning the Layout

Suppose we have the task of laying out a new factory, or a new section in an existing one. How do we start? We want to make sure that the work flows easily through the place. This involves having machines and equipment conveniently placed so that one operation follows another. We want to cut down the time and transport to a minimum. This means that the distances must be kept as short as possible. It may also mean that we have to think about cranes, passage for fork-lift trucks, and so on. We want the lighting to be right, with no dark corners but with no glare which would be trying to the eyes. We should also think about the convenience of the operators, vending machines for tea and coffee, cloakrooms, and the like.

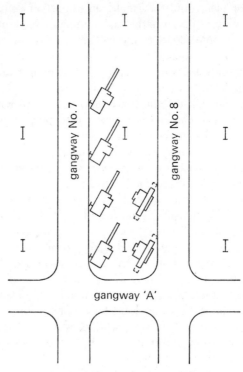

FIG. 2. *Scale model using templates*

We could never be sure of getting all this right the first time. Also we would want to bring several different people in on it—the internal transport man for the movement of material, the maintenance man for easy access to machines, and so on. These and others will have their ideas, some of which will be useful. But how do we take them all into account? Moreover, how do we try out different ways of putting them together? We can't move the machinery in, then shift it around every half-hour until we hit on the best arrangement.

A Scale Model will give us the answer here. This can show the dimensions of the room we have available, the means of access, heights, and other essential restrictions. Then we can make *templates* on the same scale, showing the plant and equipment we intend to use. We can push these around as we like, to see the effect of different layouts. Each one can be tried out in terms of the conditions discussed above. If it proves unsatisfactory, it can be changed round again and another one tried. This makes it possible to experiment with dozens of different layouts; to bring several different people in for advice; to mull over the plans until every aspect has been considered in detail. It involves no expense other than the time of the people responsible for planning the layout. And if they know their stuff, they will produce a plan which may save thousands of pounds over the next few years. This is one of the occasions when time spent in planning and experimenting with models and diagrams is fully justified. Fig. 2 shows a typical scale model.

The Outline Process Chart. When we get down a little closer to detail we shall want to show a bit more of what actually happens to the product at various stages. This is where the outline process chart makes its appearance. It is defined in the following terms:

Outline Process Chart: A process chart giving an overall picture by recording in sequence only the main operations and inspections. (BSI 3138, 1959. Glossary of terms in work study.)

This makes it possible to show how material or components enter into the production process; what operations are carried out on them; how they move from one operation to the next; where they are inspected. It does not go very far into detail of who does what or where he does it. But it is useful in highlighting possible bottlenecks once production is started up.

To simplify recording, the following symbols are available. These have been standardized so that they can be universally understood. Normally, only the first two are used in the outline process chart.

Symbol	Activity	Description
○	*Operation*	Indicates the main steps in a process, method, or procedure. Usually the part, material, or product concerned is modified or changed during the operation.
▢	*Inspection*	Indicates an inspection for quality and/or a check for quantity.
⇨	*Transport*	Indicates the movement of workers, materials, or equipment from place to place.

Symbol	Activity	Description
D	*Temporary Storage*	Indicates a delay in the sequence of events; for example, work waiting between consecutive operations, or any object laid aside temporarily without record until required.
▽	*Permanent Storage*	Indicates a controlled storage in which material is received into or issued from a store under some form of authorization, or an item is retained for reference purposes.

(BSI Glossary of terms in work study.)

These symbols should be fairly easy to understand as they more or less explain themselves. Perhaps the difference between 'Temporary Storage or Delay' and 'Permanent Storage' should be emphasized a little. The latter means that storage has been planned beforehand and products have been taken in and recorded. The former means an unplanned storage or delay, where work simply piles up between operations.

Every process chart should have a *title* and a *date*. There is nothing more irritating than to come across a bit of paper, and then to have to ask around to find which job it represents and when it was done. It should also have a clear *beginning* and an *end*, so that when it is referred to later, we know exactly which stage in the production process it covers. It is also advisable to make clear whether it is the *present* method it describes, or whether it is a *proposed* method on which changes have been worked out.

The chart should also have a *concise description* of the activity or movement represented by each symbol. Here again, present and proposed operations should be distinguished. Where appropriate, *times* and *distances* should also be included.

Fig. 3 gives an example of an outline process chart.

The Flow Process Chart. Once the general idea of a process has been obtained from an outline chart, certain aspects may call for a finer analysis. This will apply particularly to non-productive aspects, such as transportation, delays, and storage. A flow process chart can then be useful, defined as follows:

Flow Process Chart: A process chart setting out the sequence of the flow of a product or a procedure by recording all events under review, using the appropriate process chart symbols. (BSI 3138, 1959. Glossary of terms in work study.)

These charts can show what happens to the material, men, or

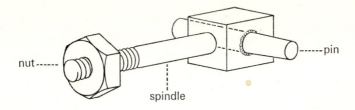

OUTLINE PROCESS CHART

Man ⎫
Material ⎬ Type   Present ⎫ Method   Date: 1 Sept '67
         ⎭   Proposed⎭

Job: Machine and assemble retaining bolt XYZ 123
Chart begins: Materials at machines
Chart ends: Final assembly

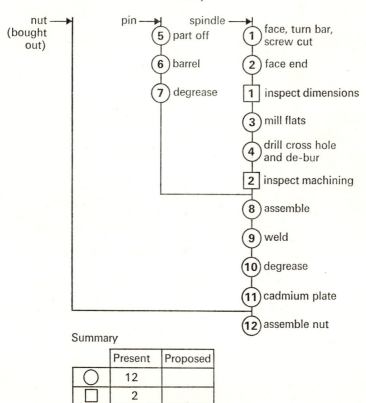

FIG. 3. *Outline process chart*

Man ⎱ Type Present ⎱ Method   Date: 2 Sept '67
Materials ⎰   Proposed ⎰
Job: Machining spindle for retaining bolt XYZ 123
Chart begins: Material on goods receiving deck
Chart ends: Component awaiting assembly order

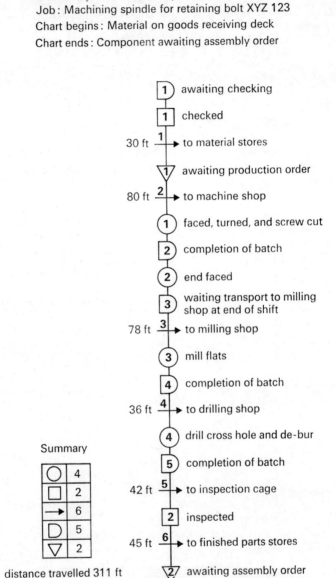

1	awaiting checking
1	checked
30 ft → 1	to material stores
1	awaiting production order
80 ft → 2	to machine shop
1	faced, turned, and screw cut
2	completion of batch
2	end faced
3	waiting transport to milling shop at end of shift
78 ft → 3	to milling shop
3	mill flats
4	completion of batch
36 ft → 4	to drilling shop
4	drill cross hole and de-bur
5	completion of batch
42 ft → 5	to inspection cage
2	inspected
45 ft → 6	to finished parts stores
2	awaiting assembly order

Summary

○	4
□	2
→	6
D	5
▽	2

distance travelled 311 ft

Fig. 4. *Flow process chart*

plant in the course of production. These should never be mixed up. Where necessary, separate charts are constructed in the same way as outline process charts. All five symbols are used and distances entered alongside transportations. Total distances are entered in the summary box. An example of a flow process chart is shown in Fig. 4.

Flow Diagrams can be used in conjunction with scale models. These show the movement of men and materials in the production process. They also show the distances in feet or yards. With the layout drawn to scale, showing the salient features of machinery, doorways, girders, etc., each operation can be plotted at the appropriate spot. Once this has been done, any unnecessary movement back and forth will show up. Similarly, we shall see if there are any areas of high traffic density, where things get in each other's way, with queueing, back-tracking, and other time-wasting delays. If we did a flow diagram for people getting to work in any large town or city, we should have an interesting example of this. Unfortunately it would only show up what everyone already knows— that our cities could be greatly improved so far as traffic and move-ment are concerned. The definition here is as follows:

A Flow Diagram is a diagram or model substantially to scale, which shows the location of specific activities carried out and the routes followed by workers, materials, or equipment, in their execution. (BSI 3138, 1959. Glossary of terms in work study.) An example of a flow diagram is shown in Fig. 5.

A further development on the same lines is the *String Diagram.* We set up our scale model on a board, showing all the equipment, doorways, and so on. We then attach a cord at the point where the production process begins. We carry this cord along the path taken by the product, sticking in a pin at each point where it stops or changes direction. This will give us a picture of the movement of the product. And if we finish up with hanks and hanks of string and dozens of pins, we shall know it is time to think again.

String diagrams are very useful for showing up where excessive transportation is taking place. Repetitive back-and-forward movement will be seen in layers of string piling up one on top of another. Long-distance movements will show up in lengths of string running from a pin in one corner to another at the other end of the board. The difference between an easy flow of production and a badly planned layout will be seen at a glance on the two string diagrams. Definition is as follows:

A String Diagram is a scale plan or model on which a thread is used to trace and measure the path of workers, material, or

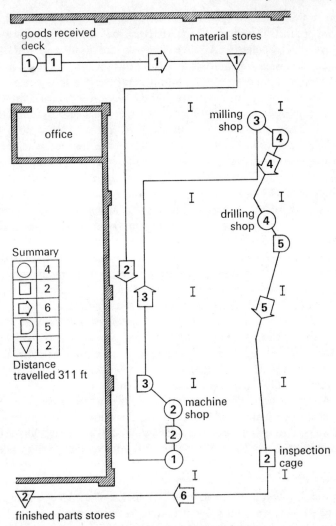

Fig. 5. *Flow diagram relating to Fig. 4*

equipment during a specific sequence of events. (BSI 3138, 1959. Glossary of terms in work study.) Fig. 6 shows an example of a simple string diagram.

The methods we have been discussing can be used for two different purposes. The first of these is to record what is happening at the moment. The second is to plan what should be done in the future. It may well be, as we have said, that the supervisory manager will not often be called in to plan the layout of a new factory in

Type: Man   Job: **Metal box** XYZ 123

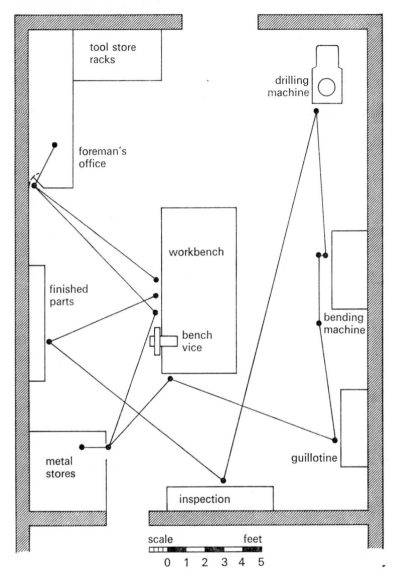

Fig. 6. *String diagram*

scale   feet

0 1 2 3 4 5

Distance: 93 ft

detail. Nevertheless, if he is on the ball, he should be thinking about how his own section is working at the moment. He might well set himself an exercise in recording what is happening there, using the methods we have been describing. With a scale model and templates, he might do the layout as it stands at present. And with a flow diagram or a string diagram, he might show how the products move through it. If his enthusiasm is still holding out, he might have a go at an outline process chart and a flow chart. This would be a useful exercise in itself. But it would almost certainly have another result as well. It would show up ways in which either the layout could be improved, or the production process streamlined.

This, of course, is where things get a bit tricky. If he shows his charts and diagrams to management and makes the suggestions that arise from them, he may do himself a bit of good. Management may accept his ideas, put them into practice, and find that the costs are well justified in increased efficiency. On the other hand, they may feel he is sticking his nose in where it isn't wanted and showing up their own inefficiency. And if his suggestions are good, practical ones, they'll feel even more hurt that they didn't think of them first themselves. Then he'll be in the doghouse good and proper. So watch your step!

Maintenance

Anything in constant use is subject to wear and tear. This applies to plant and machinery as well as shoes and socks. But how do we deal with wear and tear, and the drop in efficiency that goes with it?

There are two ways. Either we can say that the item is 'expendable', can be easily replaced, and doesn't involve heavy cost. In which case we can run it until it breaks down and then write it off. Or we can accept that the capital cost is so high that it is worth taking trouble to keep the item in operation as long as possible. In these cases, plans must be laid to anticipate wear and tear, and by a series of checks, replacements, and overhauls, to prevent breakdowns.

This is the general idea behind what is called 'Preventive Maintenance' (or planned maintenance), which is becoming more and more widely accepted in modern industry. It depends upon investigations to determine the 'life' of machines and their components, or the period during which they will run as they were designed to do. Towards the end of this 'life' their performance will begin to fall off, either through wear of the parts, fouling, failures in adjustment, or similar causes. If allowed to continue operating in this condition they will produce faulty work, and will eventually end up with a minor or a major breakdown. When this happens, several people will suffer.

Operators will be unable to earn their wages. This is serious enough in itself, but there are side-effects. If the plant is constantly breaking down, morale will suffer. The better operators will leave for other jobs where they can rely on more satisfactory working conditions. Absence and labour turnover will go up. And the supervisory manager will find that he has to deal with a constant stream of complaints and grumbles, most of which are justified.

The owners of the concern will suffer also, for non-productive time costs money. Add to this the cost of repairs, which may be expensive if the breakdown is a major one. The overall value of the business will be dropping also as the plant deteriorates. You will find this illustrated when you try to trade-in a used motor-car. You will get a better allowance if the agent knows that it has been regularly maintained and serviced.

Customers will come off badly as well, for unforeseen break-downs mean that delivery promises cannot be kept. As industry develops, these become more and more important. In a 'highly integrated' industry like motor-car production, the final product is really an assembly of a number of components. Some of these have been made in other departments, some may have been bought out from other firms. If you think of all the different bits that go into a motor-car—wheels, tyres, engine, body, electrical system, seats, and so on—you will realize what a lot of detailed planning is needed to keep the final assembly line going. If your firm is supplying a component in an industry like this, it simply cannot risk the kind of breakdown that would hold up production.

Preventive maintenance is thus becoming increasingly important. Once the life of machines or components has been ascertained, a series of checks must be planned. How these are done will depend on the equipment. In some cases, minor adjustments may be adequate; in others a complete stripping down may be required, with working parts being replaced or repaired. We cannot go into details here, but the important thing is to understand the general idea. Preventive maintenance is almost an attitude of mind, one which accepts that wear and tear happens whether you like it or not, and makes plans to prevent this holding up production. The 'knowledgeable chap' who used to come down and tinker about to get the machine going again is right out of date. We now realize that he often did more damage than he put right. A modern maintenance department works to a time-table and a plan, with mechanics who have been trained systematically to locate faults, and replace components where necessary.

Supervisory managers will find that they have to co-operate with preventive maintenance plans. This should not mean that machines are taken out of production without notice, or that they are at the beck and call of the maintenance mechanic. It should mean that they are working with another specialist department on a scheme which has a considerable long-term value. And if they appreciate the long-term value of the scheme, they will find it easier to collaborate with the specialist department.

SUMMARY

1 *What is the ideal site for a factory?*

There isn't one. Any site will present a balance of advantages and disadvantages. A town site is better from the point of view of accessibility, labour, transport, etc., but will be expensive and subject to planning restrictions. A country site may be cheaper, but will be less accessible and may present transport and labour problems.

2 *What considerations affect the type of building?*

Single-storey buildings may be cheaper, have foundations capable of supporting heavy equipment, make internal transport easier, and use natural lighting. They can, on the other hand, use up a great deal of land and be difficult to keep warm. Multi-storey buildings will be more expensive to erect but, by making better use of land, cost less per square foot of floor space. They can, however, present internal transport and access problems. They will require artificial lighting, but they may be easier to heat.

3 *What are the main factors which affect the layout of a factory?*

First, the production process and the plant and equipment it involves. Where this is heavy and bulky, the factory must virtually be laid out around it. With lighter equipment, the layout can be planned to allow for an easy flow of production, safe means of access, quick and efficient internal transport, and the convenient provision of services. At the same time, maximum use must be made of expensive floor space.

4 *What objectives should be borne in mind when planning a production flow?*

(a) Achieving maximum utilization of plant and personnel.
(b) Keeping stocks of raw material and work-in-progres sat the lowest safe level.

To some extent, these are in conflict with each other, for a shortage of material or work-in-progress could leave operators or plant with nothing to work on. Each, however, can be measured in terms of cost, and the aim should be to achieve the best balance between them.

5 *What aids are available in planning the layout of a factory?*

Scale models and templates make it easy to experiment with different layouts before committing the company to the expense of installing plant and equipment. These try-outs can be discussed with the various people involved, and modifications made according to their requirements or advice.

6 *What is an outline process chart?*

This moves away from the confines of a scale diagram to list the various events in a production process as they occur. Two symbols are used to indicate these—operation, inspection (see page 19). By the use of these, an outline process chart can give an overall picture of the main operations and inspections. (See Fig. 3.)

7 *What is a flow process chart?*

This provides for a finer analysis by recording in some detail the events shown up in the outline chart. Five symbols are used to indicate operation, inspection, transport, delay, and storage, but a description of what takes place under each is given. Times and distances are recorded under transportations and delays. (See Fig. 4.)

8 *What is a flow diagram?*

This is based on a scale drawing of the layout, and shows where the different operations are carried out. It also shows the movement of materials, operators, or equipment, between these operations. Flow diagrams are useful in showing up where these travel back and forward unnecessarily, and also the areas of high traffic density where delays may occur. (See Fig. 5.)

9 *What is a string diagram?*

This is similar to a flow diagram, but with a cord or thread used to show the movements. Pins are inserted into the scale drawing at each point where the product (or operator; but never on the same diagram) stops or changes direction. Following the string from start to finish will show whether the flow is quick and easy, or whether there are avoidable delays and diversions.

10 *What do we mean by preventive or planned maintenance?*

This is a plan of regular checks or overhauls of machinery and equipment, laid out on the 'life' of components. When carried out successfully it ensures that these are replaced or repaired before they become defective, thus avoiding unexpected faults or breakdowns.

Up to this point we have been thinking about the movement of products through the factory. We have been concerned with the buildings and the site, and the advantages and disadvantages of various types. We have been looking at the layout, making sure that one operation fits in with the next; linking up the various jobs so as to get a steady flow of production; making sure that no time or transport is wasted in moving the product from one stage to the next. This should always be the first step in planning, for it shows up the broad picture. It calls attention to any large-scale inefficiencies which, when they are put right, may lead to big savings of time and money. It is no use trying to save seconds on a detailed job if we are wasting hours moving the product around unnecessarily.

So far, however, we have paid little or no attention to the jobs done by the individual operators. The obvious next step, therefore, will be to take a closer look at these. We must now try recording what they are actually doing to the product when they are working on it. Observation and recording are always the place to begin, so out come the clip-board and the stop-watch.

The chap with the stop-watch is not a popular figure on the factory floor. He pokes his nose in where he's not wanted. He upsets everyone by trying to make out they are inefficient when they have been doing a perfectly good job of work for years. He tries to interfere in things he knows nothing about. He wants to change jobs around just to impress his bosses. He's a perfect bloody nuisance, in fact. And underneath it all, of course, what he's really trying to do is to dream up excuses to cut the piecework prices. More work for less money! That's what's really at the back of all this work study jazz.

This is perhaps a bit exaggerated, but it gives a fair idea of what a lot of people think about work study. Before we start on the subject, therefore, we should perhaps stand back a little and consider the general idea behind it. The formal definition of work study is as follows:

Work Study is a generic term for those techniques, particularly method study and work measurement, which are used in the examination of human work in all its contexts, and which lead systematically to the investigation of all the factors which affect the efficiency and economy of the situation being reviewed in order to effect improvement. (BSI 3138, 1959. Glossary of terms in work study.)

The Application of Work Study

The first point we must get hold of, therefore, is that work study is a 'technique of systematic investigation'. That is to say, it is a method of looking at any task in order to find out *how* it is being done. If you want a simple example, watch your wife setting the table. She'll fetch the tablecloth from the cupboard and spread it out. Then she'll get the plates and lay them out; then the cups and saucers; then the knives and forks, then the bread, the butter and jam; and so on. If you like, you can note down all these moves as she does them. You can even note the time each one takes. You'll finish up with a complete and detailed record of all the moves she's made while carrying out this particular task of laying the table. This is a simple, but perfectly realistic work study exercise. What harm could there possibly be in it?

Well, perhaps there's no actual harm in it, but wait a minute! By the time you've got all these moves noted down you've probably noticed that she's made one or two unnecessary journeys. She's brought the plates, then gone back for the cups and saucers. She's gone back again for the knives and forks, and then again for the bread and butter. This is all rather a waste of time, so being a perfect husband you try to be helpful. You say, 'Darling, it would save you time if you put all these things on a tray at one time, then carried them to the table and laid them out. The way you're doing it you're giving yourself a lot of extra walking back and forward for nothing.' If your wife is the perfect woman, as on the telly, she'll say, 'Oh, thank you darling. How clever you are! I never thought of that, but I'll do it your way from now on.' So in this perfect household, work study will be used to make the household jobs easier and less time-consuming.

If, however, your wife is something less than perfect, she may react rather differently. She may reply, 'All right, bighead! If you think you can teach me how to lay a table after all these years of slaving away, it's time you started doing it yourself. Sitting there spying on me and criticizing the way I run the house! Why I ever married you I can't imagine. I ought to have my head examined. And that reminds me of another thing . . .' After a few minutes of this you'll wish you'd never heard of work study, much less tried to apply it in the house.

Reactions to the Technique

This little example, we hope, brings out some of the problems of applying this 'technique of systematic investigation'. In the first place, people don't like to be spied on when they're working. In the second, the very act of studying someone at work gives him the idea that you're criticizing the way he's going about it. Thirdly, any changes which may be suggested take this criticism one stage further. Fourthly, the changes themselves mean an upset to the established routine. And fifthly, the fact that the changes have been suggested by someone else makes a chap feel he's being messed about. All of these are perfectly natural human reactions. But all of them mean that the attitude to work study is usually an unfavourable one. Work study is nothing more than a technique of systematic investigation, as we have said. In itself, it is fairly straightforward and can be understood by anyone who takes the trouble to study it. But work study usually arouses hostile emotional attitudes. And these are far more tricky to deal with, especially in a period of full employment. In fact, it is not the technique that raises the problem. It is the attitude it gives rise to on the factory floor; among operators; among management; among work study engineers; and between the lot of them at the same time.

All this affects the supervisory manager in a number of ways. First of all, he must try to get his own attitude right—to realize that this is a tool of modern management whose object is to make human effort more productive. Next, he must accept the fact that it is going to be disliked, or even resented, by many of the people under him. They're going to feel that it affects their pay packets. He's the chap who'll have to deal with this resentment, after the work study engineer has retired safely to his office. Over and above this, he must get used to the fact that he'll have to put the new methods into effect in the day-to-day working of his section. This may sound as though we're expecting a lot of the supervisory manager. But this is something we've got to keep facing up to. Functional specialists are all very well; they have their place in industry, and their scope is going to increase. But the real effectiveness of these specialists lies in the use made of their knowledge and expertise in the day-to-day working of the factory floor. And the chap on whom this depends is the supervisory manager, not the specialist. Unless he understands and appreciates what the functional specialist is trying to do, then the wages of that specialist are going down the drain.

For over a hundred years, people have been applying work

study in one way or another. Robert Owen in the early 1800s tried to make work less fatiguing in his New Lanark cotton mills. At the end of the century, F. W. Taylor designed a range of shovels, each of which could pick up a weight which was easy to lift—small ones for heavy material like iron ore, larger ones for light stuff like ashes. Frank Gilbreth and his wife Lilian studied movements and suggested a 'principle of motion economy'. Later on, Charles Bedaux introduced the idea of rating the effort put into work. Recent developments include the standardization of techniques of study, training work study engineers in these, the use of the methods in non-repetitive work, and so on.

The main objective of work study is to increase the productivity of human effort; to get more output from the same input of effort; or to get the same output from a lower input of effort. In the long run, this means greater profitability for the company, and we have already gone into the question of who benefits from this. Work study can be divided into three phases:

Method Study or *how* the task should be done:
Work Measurement or *how long* it should take:
Job Evaluation or *how much* we should pay for it.

We shall deal with these in turn.

Formal definitions are useful in getting our ideas straight. The following is the accepted definition of Method Study.

Method Study is the systematic recording and critical examination of existing and proposed ways of doing work, as a means of developing and applying easier and more effective methods and reducing costs. (BSI 3138, 1959. Glossary of terms in work study.)

In other words, we look at what is being done, we examine it critically, and try to find a better method of doing it. When we come to apply this on the job, however, it is not quite so simple as it sounds. There are several steps which must be taken, and it may help to sort out our ideas if we go into these one at a time. They are as follows:

1 We *select* the work we are going to investigate.
2 We *record* the method by which it is being done at present.
3 We *examine* the facts obtained critically and systematically.
4 We *develop* a new way which is more economical and can be applied in practice.
5 We *install* the new method as a standard procedure.
6 We *maintain* the new method by routine checks at intervals.

Each of these steps presents its problems.

Selecting the Work to be Studied

The problems involved here are of three kinds—economic, technical, and human.

The *economic* problems are concerned with the return we hope to get from the efforts of the work study engineer. In a busy factory with all sorts of jobs going, where will it be best for him to start? On a job where we could expect a large increase in production? Or one where we might get a large reduction in waste and scrap? Or one where labour costs could be cut down? These are the kinds of question which should be revolving in the mind of the up-to-date supervisory manager. And if he is really on the ball, the work study engineer should never be short of work to study. Can one imagine a situation where, when he sits down at lunch in the canteen, a supervisory manager says to him, 'Oh, I've been thinking about you. There's a job that wants looking at, down in my section. When can you come down and make a study of it?' And the work study engineer replying, 'My God, can't a chap ever get a bit of peace in this place? I'm up to my neck in the assembly shop for the next couple of weeks and you want me to come and look at one of your piddling little jobs. I should have thought I could at least rely on having my dinner without being chased round the place.' Perhaps this is a little unrealistic, but it is pleasant to think of the functional specialists being helped round the bend by supervisors, rather than the other way round.

These economic considerations should never be lost sight of. There may be cases where a small recuction in a large cost, say 1% off £100, would be more valuable than a large reduction in a small cost, say 5% off £10. It is important that the work study man should be used where his services will give the best return. For this, after all, is what higher management is interested in.

Some of the problems will also be *technical*. If the method study leads to suggestions for changes in the job, have we the necessary know-how to carry these out? Can we make the changes in plant and equipment? If we change one job in a process, how will this affect the others?

But the most serious problems will usually be *human* ones.

Suppose we start a method study of a job which now takes ten operators. We find that with a better layout it could be done just as well by seven. So we've now got three redundant operators on our hands. This will go down well in the section, won't it? Three of our mates out of a job after that damn' time study fellow started on them! We'll get the Union on to this to see it doesn't happen again, by God! A start like this means that from then on, the words 'work study' will stink. And that any attempt to look at a job will be met with hostility. But if, on the other hand, we start with the dirty unpleasant jobs and make them a bit easier and safer, we'll have a chance of building up a better attitude. Work study in general, and method study in particular, may never be exactly welcome on the factory floor. But at least there are different degrees of hostility.

This again is where the supervisory manager can play a most important part. He is the person who can give the best advice on which job to select for study. He should appreciate the kinds of return that could be expected, and he knows what the reactions on the floor are likely to be. He can also foresee the difficulties, though he should be careful not to make too much of a song and dance about these. Once he has pointed out the best jobs to start on, the next thing is to consult the people concerned and their representatives. It will be worth while to spend a good deal of time and attention on this. For if suspicions can be put to rest and the first method study carried out without rousing hostility, things are likely to go more easily in the future. As we said before, the attitudes to work study are often more important than the technique itself.

Recording What is being Done

The second step—recording what is being done—is perhaps the most important in the whole method study process. For unless the work study engineer has got every detail in the job noted in the correct sequence, he can make a first-class ass of himself when he suggests changes. He must see the job himself, for there is no substitute for direct observation. He must ask questions of as many different people as he thinks might be connected with the job. He must also check the answers he gets against one another. Obviously, one of his main sources of information will be the supervisory manager. So it's as well to start getting used to the questions you are probably going to face. What is the operator expected to do? What methods is he expected to use? What equipment does he have, and how does he use it? What material is he working on, and how does he get it? Does anybody else help him, and if so, how? Why does he do it this way and not that way? And so on, and so on.

The person who can give the most valuable information, however, is the operator himself. But this is where things can get tricky. For it is always possible that he may not be going about the job in the way he's supposed to. This may be because he's thought up little things on his own that make it easier. Little things that he'd rather keep to himself. Or it may be because of faults in his equipment or the supply of material. This is often the reason behind the complaint: 'I can't get my day in'. The operator is having to spend time on things he's not being paid for.

This mass of detailed information, in any case, can be of little use in itself. It's got to be put into some sort of shape before it makes sense, and this is where the various charts and diagrams come into the picture. They make it possible to sort out the information within an overall framework. There are various different kinds of these, some of which serve to give a general idea of what is going on and some of which go into greater detail for the various stages in the process.

We have already described:

Outline Process Charts for a broad idea of the process.

Flow Process Charts for details of what activities take place and how parts come together.

Flow Diagrams and String Diagrams for showing the movement of men and materials.

Now we must look at methods of charting the details of the jobs themselves.

To start with the simplest, any job can be broken down into 'make ready', 'put away', and 'do' operations.

Make ready and *put away* operations are concerned with the preparation and clearing-away activities for the 'do' operations. They will include provision of material, setting-up of plant and equipment, and passing on the completed product.

Do operations are those which are carried out on the product; which change its properties or characteristics, as in machining or assembly, according to what is required at that stage of the process.

It is always advisable to concentrate on the 'do' operations by shading them in on the process chart or otherwise calling attention to them. For if any of the 'do' operations can be eliminated, then the 'make ready' and 'put away' operations, including the transport they involve, will automatically disappear.

Two-handed Process Chart. In the vast majority of 'do' operations, the worker will be using his hands and arms, and in some cases, his legs and feet as well. To record these movements, some kind of chart will obviously be necessary. Those we have discussed in the preceding chapter will be useful here, and the same symbols will serve. We can make a 'Two-handed Process Chart' to record any

Present/Proposed method   Date: 3 Sept '67
Job: Assemble bolt, washer, nut, and lock nut
Chart begins: Components in position—hands empty
Chart ends: Assembly completed in work pan

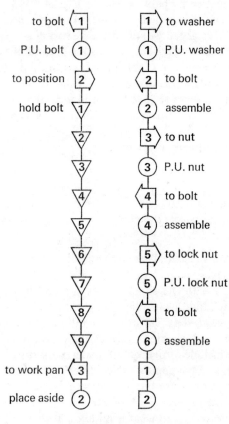

Summary

	L.H.	R.H.
◯	2	6
▷	3	6
▽	9	0
D	0	2

FIG. 7. *Two-handed process chart*

manipulative operation, the only variation being that the triangle for 'Storage' now means 'Hold'. Two columns are laid out, one for the right hand and one for the left. The symbols show what is being done by each on the same time scale. Thus, in the diagram (Fig. 7) the left hand stays at 'Hold', with the bolt in it for quite some time. The right hand, meanwhile, is putting the washer, nut, and lock-nut on to it. If the chap was also using his feet on the job we should add a further couple of columns for them. In all cases a brief description of what is happening is added alongside each symbol as in Fig. 7. The formal definition is as follows:

Two-handed Process Chart: A process chart in which the activities of a worker's hands (or limbs) are recorded in relationship to one another. (BSI 3138, 1959. Glossary of terms of work study.)

The two-handed process chart is a fairly simple one, and anyone with a general idea of method study should be able to make a shape at it. Its object is to see whether the work of the limbs is evenly balanced and whether each is being used to the best advantage. In Fig. 7, for example, it is pretty obvious that the left hand isn't doing very much. It is simply being used as a fixture to hold the bolt while the right hand does the work. Would it be worth while to design a fixture for this purpose so that both hands could be used to assemble the washer, nut, and lock-nut? This brings us to our next point, whether a more detailed investigation into a job is likely to lead to worthwhile results. This is where we are led into the finer points of method study.

Gilbreth's Classifications of Movement and the 'Therbligs'. The pioneers in this field were Frank and Lilian Gilbreth. They laid out five classifications of movement as follows:*

Fingers only	Class I
Fingers and hand	Class II
Fingers, hand, and lower arm	Class III
Fingers, hand, lower and upper arm	Class IV
Fingers, hand, lower and upper arm, and body	Class V

These classifications can be used in the more detailed study of an operation. Each one is noted along with the details of every stage in the job. If a lower classification can be substituted for a higher one, then the fatigue of the job has been cut down. A further develop-

---

* These have been adapted slightly from the original Gilbreth classifications. It will be noted that the change from each to the one above involves the movement of a joint. Thus, the knuckle comes between I and II, the wrist between II and III, the elbow between III and IV, and the shoulder between IV and V. We are indebted to Mr J. Swales of Coventry Technical College for this insight.

ment was their list of 'Therbligs'. This is simply the name 'Gilbreth' spelt backwards. They provide a kind of shorthand by which movements can be noted in detail. With them a trained motion study man can get a complete record of any manipulative job. The following list shows the 'Therbligs', each with the action it describes, the appropriate symbol, and the identifying colour.

Action	Symbol	Identifying Colour
Search	⟲	Black
Find	⟳	Grey
Select	⟶	Light grey
Transport empty	⌣	Light green
Transport loaded	⌣	Dark green
Grasp	⋂	Dark red
Release load	⌢	Light red
Position	9	Dark blue
Pre-position	8 (skittle)	Light blue
Use	∪	Purple
Assemble	#	Dark violet
Dis-assemble	⫫	Light violet
Rest	ꝑ	Orange
Inspect	0	Light brown
Plan	ρ	Dark brown
Avoidable delay	⌐	Light yellow
Unavoidable delay	⌢	Dark yellow
Hold	⌂	Gold

Therbligs are mainly used in connection with SIMO Charts, which are described below.

Advanced Work Study Methods

By this time we have moved into the land of the specialist. As we suggested above, any properly trained supervisory manager should be able to understand and make use of simple method study techniques. There comes a point, however, where the observations and recording, as well as the equipment required, become too complicated for the intelligent layman. The specially trained work study engineer now moves in on the job and the layman stands aside. It is essential, however, that the present-day supervisory manager should have some idea of what the expert is doing. Only then can he make adequate use of his service. We shall thus spend a moment on the more advanced techniques and try to give a general outline of them.

Many of them make use of photographic aids. Still pictures are useful for recording the present situation. If taken from the correct angle, they will show how the operators and equipment stand in relation to each other. They can also be examined by several people at different times. This overcomes the disadvantage of an on-the-spot observation by one person at a particular moment of time. Cine films have the added advantage of showing movement and they can also be adapted to show timings.

There are, however, limitations in the use of photographic aids. In the first place, they are expensive, both in equipment and in time. Secondly, they involve the use of cameras and spotlights, and the workshop may become cluttered up with wires and cables all over the place. Thirdly, they make the whole work situation artificial, so that people may not always behave naturally or as they normally do on the job. There may also be the reactions we mentioned above, the feeling of being spied on or having one's actions put under the microscope. These limitations should always be borne in mind before diving off the deep end into advanced motion study.

The following examples may illustrate some of the methods:

Memomotion. A camera can be set up to cover a job and timed to take a picture at regular intervals. These might be every thirty seconds or every minute, and it would continue to do so throughout the working day. When the film has been developed it is run at normal speed. The result, of course, is a bit unnatural, with operators jerking about like an early movie of the Keystone Kops. Nevertheless, it gives a fair idea of what is happening and will show periods of inactivity. This kind of study is useful when several operators are working as a team.

The Simultaneous Motion Cycle Chart (SIMO Chart). This starts with a cine film of the operator doing the job. Included in the picture is a Wink counter, running at 2,000 to the minute. When the film is analysed, these Winks give the time for each Therblig. Jobs can be studied in great detail by this method, using Therbligs. It is, however, expensive and would only be justified where there are long

4

runs on similar products. In such cases, small savings in the cycle
time of fast movements might make it worth while.

Cyclegraphs and Chronocyclegraphs. This is a further development of cine photography. Small lights are attached to the operator's
hands, and the task is filmed. If the lights are left on continuously, a
series of white lines shows the movements of the hands. This is known
as the *cyclegraph*, and gives a 'movement pattern' for the task.
Different movement patterns can then be compared. A further
development is the *chronocyclegraph*, where the lights on the hands
flick on and off at controlled speeds of ten to thirty times a second.
These flashes show up as pear-shaped dots on the film and make it
possible to add a 'time pattern' to the movement pattern.

SUMMARY

1 *What is work study?*

Work study is first of all a technique of observation and recording. It
can be used to examine systematically the manner in which any task is
being done. This leads to a review of the methods used on the job and
usually throws up ideas on how it could be made simpler and easier.

2 *What are the problems in the application of work study?*

Mainly the emotional reactions of the people being studied. Work
study carries an implication of criticism that the job is not being done
efficiently. Any changes proposed as a result may thus be resented. There
is, moreover, a suspicion that management is going to benefit more from
these changes than the worker. The supervisory manager has to bear the
brunt of the hostility which often arises from work study investigations.

3 *What are the subdivisions of work study?*

    (a) *Method Study* or the investigation of *how* the job should be done.
    (b) *Work Measurement* or the calculation of *how long* it should take.
    (c) *Job Evaluation* or working out *how much* should be paid for it.

4 *Are there any problems in selecting which job should be studied?*

There are *economic* problems concerned with the likely return in
increased efficiency for the time and money spent on work study. There
are *technical* problems concerned with whether recommendations can be
put into effect. But most important are the *human* problems which arise
out of the reactions of people to work study investigations. Every effort
must be made to start on a job which will not arouse suspicion and
hostility.

5 *How do we set about recording what is being done?*

Information can be gathered from the operator himself, from the supervisory manager, and from anyone else in contact with the job. It is important, however, that this information be organized into a suitable framework. Useful classifications for this purpose are *Make ready*, *Do*, and *Put away* operations.

6 *What is a two-handed process chart?*

This is a means of noting down what an operator does with his hands (or limbs). Columns are laid out for the right and left hands (also legs if used). These show how much use is being made of each hand (or limb) in relation to the other. (See Fig. 7.)

7 *What is the significance of Frank and Lilian Gilbreth?*

They provided five classifications of finger, hand, lower and upper arm, and body movements. Also a series of symbols for recording movements in a form of shorthand, the Therbligs.

8 *What do we mean by advanced work study methods?*

These can only be used effectively by trained specialists, as distinct from the simpler methods which the supervisory manager should be able to master. They depend largely on the use of photographic aids and include Memomotion, SIMO Charts, chronocyclegraphs, etc.

Problems may arise when there are several people working together on a job. One has to wait for another to finish his bit of the task. Another cannot begin until the first two have completed their parts. Time can be wasted with this sort of waiting around. This kind of

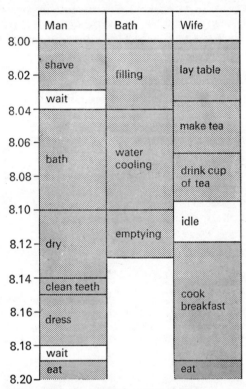

	Man	Bath	Wife
8.00	shave	filling	lay table
8.02			
	wait		
8.04			make tea
8.06		water cooling	
8.08	bath		drink cup of tea
8.10			idle
8.12	dry	emptying	
8.14	clean teeth		cook breakfast
8.16	dress		
8.18	wait		
8.20	eat		eat

Fig. 8. *Multiple activity chart*

job can be very difficult to record, but a Multiple Activity Chart can be useful here. This is defined as follows:

A Multiple Activity Chart is one in which the activities of more than one subject (worker, machine, or equipment) are each recorded on a common time scale to show their relationship. (BSI 3138, 1959. Glossary of terms in work study.)

Vertical lines are allocated to each worker or piece of equipment. A common time scale runs down the side. Blocks are ruled off in each column as the situation develops, and each block is labelled according to the activity it represents. In this way, idle time quickly shows up in blank spaces in the column. If the chart shows a lot of these blank spaces then the question immediately presents itself: 'Have we too many men on this job?' If it could be arranged so as to make effective use of this waiting time, perhaps the job could be done by a smaller group. A certain amount would depend on the operator's rate of work, but we shall leave this until we deal with rating in the chapter on Work Measurement. (See Fig. 8.)

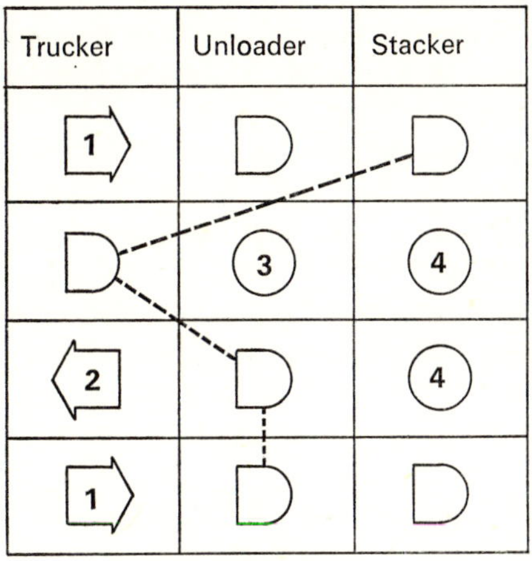

1 to stores
2 from stores
3 unloading
4 . stacking

FIG. 9. *Gang chart*

Another use for the multiple activity chart is where an operator is running a bank of machines. He starts up one, sets it for a certain run, then starts up the next, and so on. By the time he has them all running, the first machine stops and has to be re-set. If the times for these can be fitted in together, it is possible to keep this operation going very efficiently. A similar situation can arise with maintenance work.

A less accurate method of recording a number of interlinked operations is the *Gang Chart*. This follows the same general idea as the multiple activity chart, but uses the five symbols already described. The operators involved are put in vertical columns, with a time scale on the side. Fig. 9 shows this kind of chart for the loading and unloading of a lorry. It will be seen that of the three people involved, one is unoccupied in each of the operations recorded. This immediately raises the question of whether the number could be cut down.

Critical Examination

Going back for a moment to the list of steps in work study (page 34), we have now dealt with the *select* and *record* stages. We have picked out a job to be studied, having regard to the economic, technical, and the important human considerations. We have got a detailed record of what is being done, using the appropriate charts and other methods. Now we come to the next stage, which is to have a closer look at what is being done.

This is where the backroom boy really comes in. He can take time to go over what has been recorded and make a critical examination of it. He will have no preconceived ideas about 'the way we've always done the job'. He can ask awkward questions, taking a sceptical attitude to every aspect of the facts. He can experiment with different methods, without worrying at the moment whether they would be accepted on the job. It doesn't matter whether some of his ideas don't work out. The main point is that he should try as many as possible in the hope of getting one that does. He goes over the whole thing logically, looking at it from every point of view in turn. He questions, who does what? Where does he do it? When does he do it? Why does he do it? And how does he do it? These questions can be put into a framework for easy reference on the following lines:

Critical Examination Sheet*

Description of Element
Project Details   *Date*

1	2	3	4
Purpose			
What is achieved?	Is it necessary? Yes/No. If Yes, why?	What else could be done?	What should be done?
Place			
Where is it being done?	Why there?	Where else could it be done?	Where should it be done?

* Currie, R. M. *Work Study*. Pitman (1963)

Description of Element
Project Details   *Date*

1	2	3	4
Sequence			
When is it done?	Why then?	When else could it be done?	When should it be done?
Person			
Who does it?	Why that person?	Who else could do it?	Who should do it?
Means			
How is it done?	Why that way?	How else could it be done?	How should it be done?

Going from left to right on the form, a logical sequence will be seen. First of all, study the record from each point of view (column 1). Then consider the reasons (column 2). Then think about alternatives (column 3). Then reach a decision about the best method (column 4).

Points to Remember

While the backroom boy is going through all this, he will be applying some general ideas. The first of these arises out of the question: 'Is it necessary?' If this gets a 'no' answer, then the result is obvious enough. The job can be done away with. What happens to the chap who's been doing it for the past few years, of course, is another problem. Do we make him redundant? This would have been a tragedy a few years ago, but nowadays the Redundancy Payments Act softens the blow a little. Do we find him another job? If there is a suitable one going, the company will normally try to do so. And if he is a reasonable chap, as most are, he'll take it—so long as his pocket or his pride doesn't suffer. These are questions where the supervisory manager will find himself dealing with the Personnel Department. And if each can work on the problem intelligently, it will be settled without too much upset.

There are, however, other general ideas that come up, particularly under the 'How' heading. Remember that what we are trying to do is to make the job easier and less time-consuming. We should therefore try to make the movements as easy and natural as we can. If you can remember this little rhyme, you will know what to look for:

Keep the movements natural, a finger not an arm,
To switch the blessed job around and keep it out of harm.
But what about your other hand? It's easier done with two.
So use them simultaneously and see what they can do.
Make all your moves symmetrical and keep them in the swing.
Make both sides go together too, the rhythm is the thing.
The job becomes a habit then, at least we hope it will,
With every movement natural, it's money in the till.

This will remind you of the 'Principles of Motion Economy' which have been set out in other texts on the subject. They are:

1 *Minimum movements.* Using the lowest of the Gilbreth Classifications (see page 39).
2 *Simultaneous movements.* Both hands working at the same time, each performing a similar task, beginning and ending together.
3 *Symmetrical movements.* Both arms moving on either side of an imaginary centre line through the body, the task of one being the mirror-image of the other.
4 *Natural movements.* Limbs moving easily in accordance with the anatomy of the body, free of restriction.
5 *Rhythmical movements.* Building up to an automatic speed for the operation, in a pattern of limb movements.
6 *Habitual movements.* Where trained operators will have developed repetitive movements which fall into a habit.
7 *Continuous movements.* Smooth, free-swinging movements, without abrupt changes of direction, are less tiring than erratic ones in confined spaces.

These principles, of course, can only be applied when the working area has been properly laid out. Here is another rhyme to help keep this clear.

He reached for the spanner; it wasn't in place.
So think of the layout of this working space.
He needed components, but nothing was there.
He stretched out his hand and encountered thin air.
He can't see the gauges—they just need a glance.
They should have been placed where he'd see them at once.
He's got to reach over to pick up the screws.
Why weren't they placed where they're easy to use?
His left hand sits idle to hold the job neat.
There should be a fixture he'd work with his feet.

When jobs are completed he carts them away.
Why not drop them down through a chute to a tray?
He stands up all day and gets aches in his feet.
It would save his poor corns if you'd give him a seat.
He picks up a gauge, then checks with a rule.
He'd have saved a whole move with a two-in-one tool.

Maximum working area for right hand movement from shoulder

Normal working area for left hand movement from elbow

FIG. 10 *Normal and maximum working area*

This little bit of nonsense covers the points a supervisory manager should be on the lookout for in the individual working area.

1 There should be a place for everything the operator needs on the job—tools, gauges, portable equipment, etc. All these should be replaced at once, so that they can be picked up when they are wanted.

2 Components should be delivered to prearranged spots at the work station, in suitably designed containers, where both hands can grasp the bits without looking.

3 Anything he needs to look at should be positioned where it can be seen without turning the head.

4 Tools and components should be placed within the 'Normal Working Area' where hands and arms can reach easily, and certainly not outside the 'Maximum Working Area'. (See Fig. 10.)

5 Where possible, holding devices should be used in which the job can be fixed, leaving the hands free. These can be operated by foot pedals, while both hands are working on the job.

6 Disposal of completed parts should be arranged by chutes, 'drop deliveries', ejectors, or other devices which simplify the 'put away' part of the job.

7 The space the operator works in should be as comfortable as possible, with proper lighting, a well-designed and fitted chair, and a bench-top at which he can either stand or sit.

8 Two or more tools should be combined wherever possible and power tools used when practicable. This cuts down fatigue and unnecessary picking up and laying down.

During this critical examination stage, all these general ideas will be applied to the job as it has been recorded. Its limitations will thus come to light and improvements will suggest themselves. Out of this brainstorming process a new method will emerge. So we find ourselves moving imperceptibly on to the next step.

Developing and Installing the New Method

By now the work study man will have an answer to the 'What', 'Where', 'When', 'Who', and 'How' questions. There will still be many details to be worked out, however, before the new scheme is finally working. If it is being put into effect alongside existing operations, how will they be affected? In a jobbing or small-batch production shop, this may not arise. One process can be reorganized without interfering with the others. But in a large-batch or flow production shop, the whole layout may have to be reconsidered. Items of plant and machinery may have to be moved around and individual work stations redesigned. The technical practicabilities of the new scheme will have to be proved, and outside help may be needed for this.

All the aids discussed in Chapter 2 will be useful here. And the supervisory manager must be in on everything from the beginning. His advice should be the most valuable for anticipating difficulties in day-to-day working. He should also be relied on for the ideas which help to get the new process run in. It has been said that this is the stage where everybody must participate if you want success. There should, therefore, be the fullest consultation with all concerned—operators, shop stewards, trade union officials, the lot. Failure to carry them with you means that you will not get 100% value from the new scheme. The key figure in all this must be the supervisory manager.

The actual installation of the new method is really the job of the production people. They will have to consider the following points:

1 Design of the tools and equipment required by the proposed new operation.
2 Purchase of the necessary plant.
3 Arrangement of training programmes for the operators.
4 Decision on a redundancy policy if this is required.
5 Phasing of the installation in appropriate stages.

When the new process begins to run, however, the supervisory manager will have his hands full. Production may take time to build up to the level expected. Retraining of operators and fitting them into the new scheme of production will involve many headaches. There may be problems of pay and allowances while learning the new job. The final time study values for payment-by-results schemes will still have to be agreed. Special care will be required where groups of operators are involved. These are often dependent on one another for the flow of work. If a previous operation's rate of output is affected by the change, this may prevent a subsequent group from working at its normal pace. Here the work study engineer should explain what is happening to all concerned and try to obtain their co-operation.

Training, of course, is essential if the scheme is to run smoothly. One must remember, however, that maximum speed must build up with practice. Time can be saved if jobs are broken down and modern training methods used. But the 'learning curve' must always be borne in mind, and time allowed for maximum speed to be attained. This point is discussed further in Chapter 9.

Maintaining the New Method

Nothing ever works out exactly to plan. This may sound depressing, but it is real life. For sustained success, therefore, any new scheme requires checking from time to time to ensure that it is being correctly operated. Changes may come about for various reasons. Operators may adapt the methods as they get used to them and have new ideas. Some of these will be good and should be carried on. Some will not be so good and must be stopped before they develop into a habit. This is particularly important with regard to safety. It may speed up the job to leave the guard off, but the extra output is not worth a damaged hand or arm. Materials or components may be changed. This again may affect the methods on the job, so that each new item should be checked as it is introduced. Equipment will deteriorate with use, and the running repairs may involve some changes in the method. Normal labour turnover will introduce new operators who must be trained to the required standard. Minor changes in design will alter details of the process. The supervisory manager, as the man on the spot, must keep his eye on all these.

This is another example of the need for close collaboration between the functional specialist—in this case the work study engineer—and the supervisory manager. At regular intervals they should look over the work of the section together. They should check schemes that have been running for some time against the layout and specification. They should see whether the tools, movements, and other elements are being used according to what was laid down. Where improvements have been devised by the shop floor, credit should be given.

Organization and Methods

Most organizations nowadays make use of work study on the factory floor. It may not always be taken to its logical conclusion in work measurement, but one or other of the techniques outlined above can be seen in most engineering works. There are, however, other fields in which they can be applied: in office or administrative work, for example. And this is where the term 'Organization and Methods' has come into use. 'O and M', as it is commonly called, is simply the use of these methods of investigation in non-productive departments.

Mechanization has already made itself felt in the office, of course. The typewriter, the teletype, and the accounting machine have taken the place of the handwritten letter, the day-book, and the ledger. What goes on in the office, however, has not always been studied as a sequence of operations. And sometimes there has been a tendency for processes to be duplicated, for extra copies, forms, and returns to be asked for. What happens to all these extra copies, forms, and returns is not always clear. And in some cases they may never be referred to again. They have, nevertheless, to be classified and filed, thus piling up unproductive work and adding to the cost.

When the movement of documents is charted on a flow diagram, these inefficiencies will come to light. From studies of this kind, improvements in the layout of offices make it possible for one piece of paper to pass quickly through a series of operations, thus making extra copies unnecessary. Mechanical aids in the form of pneumatic tubes, conveyors, or endless chains with baskets, can speed up the process. Work loads can be balanced, unproductive operations cut out, and the whole process brought under control. Considerable reductions in overhead cost have thus become possible.

There is, however, a further possible development, known as 'data processing'. Each individual bit of information can be recorded on a punched card or, by electronic means, on a tape. 'Banks' of data can thus be built up, from which summaries or analyses or comparisons can be drawn out by 'programming' the equipment. This, in very simple terms, is how a computer works. It has a large store of data in the shape of individual employee records, rates of pay and bonus, sales and purchase transactions, and so on. When the programme has been started up, the computer makes the correct selection from these data, working in microseconds. It can thus produce the wage and bonus calculations, the monthly accounts, the figures of production efficiency, or any other analyses that may be required, in a fraction of the time it would take clerks to work them out. Even though he may not understand the details, the supervisory manager should grasp the general idea of data processing. For it is likely that sooner or later he may find himself arguing with a computer. And while it may seem very fast and impressive, he should always remember that a computer is essentially a very stupid machine. It can do simple sums very quickly indeed, but it can only answer the questions that have been put to it. And if you ask a computer a silly question, it will give you a silly answer.

Work Measurement in the Office

If office work can be method studied and timed, will the next step be to put the clerks and typists on piecework? There are some jobs, such as audio-typing, where this would be perfectly possible. There are others, of course, where work measurement could not be applied. You could hardly pay the pretty girl on the reception desk, for example, at so much a smile. It might be thought worth while to install an efficiency bonus or a merit-rating scheme, based on measured output targets, in an office. This, of course, would raise all the problems we referred to on page 32. It might, nevertheless, be worth considering, for where measurement can be introduced into work, standards can be laid down. An individual's performance can then be judged on these standards, and not on whether the boss likes his—or her—face. In some ways this makes the supervisory manager's job easier, though in others it may make it more difficult. In industry, however, we are using other people's money in plant and equipment, to produce goods or services which the customer thinks are worth the price. It is not a bad idea, therefore, to bring this general idea of value for money into every hole and corner of the organization.

SUMMARY

1 *How do we record jobs where several people are working together?*

Multiple Activity Charts or Gang Charts make it possible to record jobs of this nature. They will show up waiting time when one operator is unoccupied while another is finishing his part of the task. A study of these charts will lead to a better integration of the individual parts into the total job.

2 *Once an existing job has been recorded by work study techniques, what is the next step?*

The next step is to make a critical examination of what is being done. This involves asking: Who does what? Where does he do it? When? Why? and How? Then the reasons for these are questioned and alternatives considered. From this will develop a new method which should be experimented with, to test its practicability and acceptability.

3 *What points should be borne in mind during the critical examination?*

(a) Whether the job could be done away with and, if so, what happens to the operator.
(b) Whether time or effort could be saved by making the movements easier and more natural.
(c) Whether the layout of the work place could be improved by making things easier to reach and the operator more comfortable.

4 *What are the problems of installing a new method?*

Whether it involves changes in the layout or the production plan, and whether these are practicable. Design and purchase of any new plant and equipment. Consultation with operators and representatives over the changes, and their possible effect on earnings. Training of operators and working-up to the required speeds.

5 *Are there any problems in maintaining a new method in operation?*

There are several, arising from adaptation by operators as they develop skill; changes in materials or components; running repairs to equipment; the introduction of new labour; changes in design. Any new method should be periodically checked to ensure that it is working to specification.

6 *What do we mean by the term 'Organization and Methods'?*

'Organization and Methods', or 'O and M', means the application of work study methods of investigation to non-productive operations, such as office or administrative work. Movement of documents, individual work loads, sequence of operations can be studied, and where unnecessary delays or repetitions show up, these can be remedied. Data-processing techniques which can select or analyse information by electronic means are a further development.

CHAPTER 5 | **Work Measurement—or How Long should it Take?**

Let us come back for a moment to the domestic applications of work study. Imagine that you've sorted out the job of laying the table. Your wife is now putting everything she needs—cups, saucers, knives, forks, and all the rest—on to a tray. She carries the tray to the table and lays them out. With your help, now that you've got a grasp of the principles of method study, she's saving herself a lot of time and effort. Laying the table doesn't take anything like as long as it did before you started to help. What a wonderful chap you are! Practically the perfect husband. But there's a nasty little question lurking in the background. How long should it take her to lay the table now?

Timing a Job

Perhaps you think this is a simple matter to decide. Now that you've got the method sorted out, all you need is a stop-watch to time the operation. You sit there watching her on the job. You click the stop-watch on when she starts, and you click it off when she finishes. There you are—three minutes exactly! That's the time it should take. Surely that's all there is to it? Well, not quite, for there are a few complications.

Suppose, for example, that your small daughter takes over and lays the table tomorrow evening. Would you expect her to do it in three minutes? If you did, you'd have a lot of smashed china around! You'd soon be complaining about the cost of buying new plates and dishes if you expected a little girl to work at that speed. She hasn't got the skill or the muscular co-ordination of a grown-up housewife. So here's a factor we have to take into account in our timing of jobs. We'll call it a *skill factor* and come back to it later.

Now, think of another point. There's your wife laying the table, and there are you sitting with your stop-watch checking the time. (This is a really modern family, making use of all the up-to-date methods of increasing efficiency in the home.) When she's finished, you say, 'Darling, you're a bit slow tonight. This job only took you three minutes last night. But tonight you've taken nearly three and a half to set out exactly the same lot of dishes and cutlery.' In this modern family, with the perfect husband and wife and all that jazz, she'll answer, 'Oh darling, I wonder what's gone wrong. Perhaps I wasn't working as hard as I was last night—not putting enough effort into it.' If she's less than the perfect wife—but no! We'd better leave that to your imagination, if it's not already overworked by this perfect family.

There are two points here. One we have already dealt with: the emotional reactions of anyone who's being observed. These are likely to be more heated when the stop-watch is used, for this carries the implied criticism that he isn't working hard enough. No one can fail to resent the idea that another person thinks he is slacking on the job. So here is another example where the reaction to work study technique may be more important than the technique itself.

The other point is a new one. Yesterday, your wife was full of beans, going about the jobs with lots of energy, and getting through the housework in record time. Today she's got a pain in her tummy, she feels lousy, and she's dragging herself around thinking she'd give anything for a nice lie-down. It's no wonder that everything takes longer than it did yesterday. She just can't summon up the effort she was putting into the job. So here we have another factor we must take into account in timing jobs. We'll call it the *effort factor* and return to it later.

This should make clear some of the complications about deciding how long a task should take. Before we go into detail, we could list these briefly:

1 *The emotional reactions of the person being timed.* He may resent the implied criticism that he's not working at his usual pace, and retaliate by stopping every now and then to argue the toss or fiddle around and generally making it as difficult as he can for the chap with the stop-watch.

2 *The method used on the job.* This must be absolutely standard to the last detail. We are assuming that it has been worked out beforehand by a proper method study. We must then make sure that the operator sticks to it exactly. Method study must always come before work measurement.

3 *The skill of the operator.* This again must be standard. But how do you set a standard? The principle here is to take a qualified operator of 'average' skill, which raises problems of its own.

4 *The effort being put into the job.* Here again this must be standard. We don't want the operator to be bashing away at a speed he couldn't keep up for more than ten minutes, or working so fast that he can't keep the quality up to standard.

On the other hand, we don't want him slacking on the job. Once more the principle is that he should be working at 'average effort'. But what is 'average effort'?

Problems of Work Measurement

As we have already stressed, it is important to get the general ideas clear before getting down to their detailed application. And in the case of work measurement, this is especially true. A great deal of argument centres round the timing of jobs, for obvious reasons, some of which are tied up with payment. Money is always a hot subject, and the rate for the job depends on its timing, directly or indirectly. At the moment, however, we want to keep clear of these complications and concentrate on the general idea. If we can do this, the principles of work measurement shouldn't be difficult to grasp.

In your ordinary day-to-day life you depend a lot on work measurement, though you may never have thought about it. You know how long it takes you to get up in the morning, to shave and dress and have your breakfast. You know how long it takes to get to work and back again in the evening, to change your clothes, to have a bath, and so on. You know also how long it takes your wife to do these things and possibly the children as well. If you didn't have any idea about these timings, you'd never be able to plan your day.

Of course in these activities there's a margin of error in your timings. You take it for granted that when your wife's got a new hair-do, it'll take her longer to get ready; that your children will waste time playing around. And the idea of running your personal life by a series of stop-watch timings may seem rather revolting. So, it probably is. But when, as in production industry, we're concerned with making economic use of expensive plant and labour, are we justified in using these methods? This is really the nub of the question, and we have to face up to it.

Work measurement will never be popular on the factory floor. It reduces the chap on the job to something less than human. You've only got to think about applying it in the home to realize this. You couldn't possibly imagine your wife as a kind of mindless machine, going about her jobs according to the methods you'd laid down, on a fixed time-table. If you can, then you won't stay married very long! So, are we justified in using these techniques during working hours? If we are thinking in economic terms, as we must in industry, the answer is 'Yes' without any argument. But if we're thinking in human terms, the answer's not so simple.

We have here a clash between two points of view, the economic and the human. And once again, the supervisory manager is in the front line. He can't close his eyes to one or the other. If he thinks only in economic terms, he'll stir up so much ill-feeling that he'll lose control of his section. If he thinks purely in human terms, he won't get the output that's expected of him. How he works out a compromise between the two is something he must tackle for himself. It won't be easy. But if he ever imagined that factory-floor supervision was easy, he shouldn't have taken on the job. All we can do here is to set out the problem; to describe the techniques and their application on the one hand; and to suggest the reactions on the other. With a grasp of both, some supervisors seem to manage all right. All we can do is to hope that if you think it out from first principles, you'll be one of these.

The Skill Factor

Work measurement depends on setting accurate standards for a number of factors. The first of these concerns the method of doing the job. We shall take this for granted, hoping that the previous chapter has explained how method study can economize time and effort. We shall assume that a satisfactory way of doing the job has been worked out and that the operator is making use of it. With this method factor out of the way, let us now look at the Skill Factor.

In any shop there will be variations in skill. At one end of the scale we shall find a few operators who seem to have magic fingers. Either by natural dexterity or long practice, they can fit everything deftly into place; a flick of the wrist secures it, and a smooth, controlled motion shifts it around. At the other end of the scale, there will be a few ham-handed ones, who have to go over everything again to get it right. Nothing ever fits properly for them, and they have to spend twice as long fiddling with controls. These are the two extremes of skill on the job, and to take either of them as a standard would soon lead to trouble. If we timed the chaps at the top end of the scale, we should have a very tight standard which most people couldn't reach. If we timed those at the bottom, we should have a loose time that wouldn't represent a proper day's work.

The answer, of course, is to avoid these extremes and take someone in the middle of the scale. We want to set a standard for the average qualified operator. This shouldn't be difficult in practice, for every supervisory manager will have an idea of the range of skill in his section. He should be able to pick out someone with the 'average' amount, and take him as the standard. This perhaps sounds as though we're making it all a bit too easy, for there are all sorts of different jobs and different kinds of skill. As a matter of practical experience, however, it's fairly simple and straightforward. Any experienced supervisory manager who's been in charge of a section for any time, should be able to say, 'If you want an example of average skill in this section, Joe's about right. He's not so quick as Charlie, but he's a good deal better than Harry. Yes, I reckon Joe's your man.' Here again, the supervisory manager has a key part to play.

The Effort Factor

Now we come to the question of how hard the chap is working. Here again it is possible to think of a scale, with someone at the top sweating his guts out, and someone at the bottom taking it too damned easy. We want someone in the middle, who's putting a 'normal' or average effort into it. This is where we come up against the problem of rating. First of all, we've got to get an idea of what 'normal' or average effort is. A trained work study man can recognize this. He has a standard in mind which is neither so fast that an operator couldn't be expected to keep it up, nor so slow that it represents slacking on the job. A standard which used to be quoted was a man walking at a speed of three miles an hour. This represents a fairly brisk walk, neither hurrying nor sauntering along.

Once the idea of 'normal' effort has been grasped, it must be expressed as a figure on a scale. The most frequently used is 100. If an operator seems to be going faster than normal, increases of 5 points at a time are added to this figure. If he seems to be going slower than normal, the figure is reduced by steps of five at a time. There are other scales in use, some of which are based on 80 points, some on 133 points, and others on 1·00 for normal effort. The general idea remains the same, however, and Fig. 11 shows how these scales are related to each other. Ratings above and below 'normal' effort are given higher or lower values on each scale.

Effort rating will always be a tricky point in work measurement. It involves an estimate, or a judgment by one person on the work of another. How can we be sure that this judgment is objective and not just a personal opinion? Well, we can never be absolutely sure, for there are no fixed units of measurement in this game. We don't have to argue about the size or weight of things, for we have accepted units, like feet and inches or pounds and ounces, with which to measure. When different people use these units of measurement, they come to the same answer. But when a work study man says that a job is being done at 'normal' effort, how can we check his statement?

There is only one way to do it. This is to get another work study man to rate the same job quite separately and independently. If he comes up with the same figure as the first one, then we can at least be sure that both are working to the same standard. This really is as far as we can go, in spite of all that has been said or written about

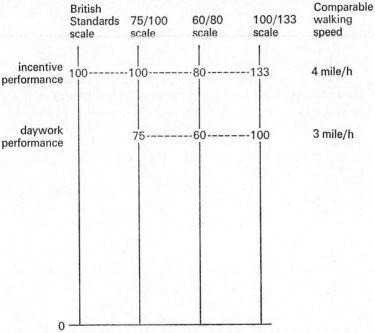

Fig. 11. *Comparison of rating scales*

accurate standards. In actual practice, however, it is quite far enough for ordinary working. Work study men are trained in rating by means of films running at set speed, with standards based on internationally agreed tests. They are taken off the job periodically and their standards checked by trial ratings. If they vary more than a certain amount, they go back for retraining. In a well-organized work study department there is very little variation in standards. This may not be the last word on the matter, but it should be enough to show how this effort factor can be dealt with.

The Relaxation Allowance

There are, however, one or two other points to be taken into account. If the work is heavy and physically tiring, can we judge it on the same basis as a light, sitting-down job? Obviously not! We have to allow time for the operator to recover unless we want him to go home a physical wreck at the end of the day. This brings us to the Relaxation Allowance, which is an estimate of the time necessary for the operator to recover from the stress of the job. It can be expressed as a percentage of the time taken. This percentage is added to each element in the cycle. Thus, in a heavy, fatiguing job we could say that a chap has to rest 30% or even 50% of the time. At this rate he'll go home no more than healthily tired. We could also say that the chap on the light, sitting-down job only needs to rest 10% of the time.

There are, of course, other things that come into the Relaxation Allowance. Different kinds of job impose different kinds of strain. Apart from the heavy fatiguing work just mentioned, there are jobs which involve awkward posture, stooping, or bending. There are awkward movements as well, which we may not be able to get rid of, reaching over and under things. There is the strain of watching dials or gauges all day; working in very hot or cold conditions; noise; smells, and so on. There are what are called 'personal needs'. (This just means going to the lavatory at necessary intervals.) These can all be included as a percentage in the Relaxation Allowance.

The Unit of Work

Now that we have got the method, skill, effort, and relaxation reduced to a standard, how do we express our measurement of the job? We need some kind of unit, so that we can say, 'This job counts for so many units, but this other counts for twice as many.' But if we are considering how long a job should take, surely the common measures of time—hours or minutes—are good enough? Well, they are, in a way. But there's a snag. We've rather messed these units about with all this chat about effort and relaxation, haven't we? We can't use the ordinary minute any more. We need a new kind of unit and this is known as the *standard minute*.

Suppose we have timed a chap and found that the job he's working on takes exactly ten minutes by the stop-watch. It's a fairly heavy job, and he's worked without stopping all the time we've been watching him. If we value this job at ten minutes, we're paying no attention to the fatigue, personal needs, and all the other things which should be included in the Relaxation Allowance. All right, so we add 20% for these allowances and this brings our time up to twelve minutes. But are these minutes by the stop-watch, ordinary minutes of time? No, they're not, for we've added this percentage to them. They've now become a different kind of minute, which is the 'standard minute'. And this is the unit which is most widely used in work measurement. The 'standard minute' consists of so much work content and so much Relaxation Allowance.

It is very important to grasp the general idea of a 'standard minute'. The first point to get hold of is that it is not a measure of time. It is a measure of work. Its definition is on the following lines:

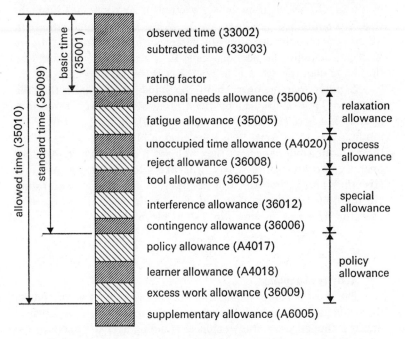

Numbers in brackets are taken from *Glossary of terms in work study*
B.S.I. Publication 3138 : 1959

FIG. 12. *Diagrammatic build-up of a time value*

A standard minute is the amount of work done by an operator of average skill working on a satisfactory method, at normal effort.

Fig. 12 shows work content and allowances.

This measure can be applied to a variety of jobs. We could say, for example, that getting up in the morning, shaving, and dressing represents twenty standard minutes; setting the table represents five; washing the breakfast dishes for two people ten; and so on. All of these jobs would have been timed and rated by the methods described above.

If you feel you have got the hang of this method of measurement, then the question of how long a job should take should no longer

bother you. You should see how the standard minute can be applied
in all sorts of different ways. It can be used to lay out a programme
of work, for if an operator is on the job for eight hours, we can give
him eight 'standard hours' of work to do. (A standard hour is simply
sixty standard minutes.) We can check up how efficiently he has been
working; for if he completes his eight standard hours in eight hours
by the clock, he has done all we wanted. If he completes his eight
standard hours in seven hours by the clock, he has done more than
we asked him. (The question of whether we reward him for this, we
shall put off until the next chapter.) If he has taken nine hours by
the clock, then this work is below the standard we expect.

A point to remember about the standard minute is that the
Observed Time multiplied by the Rating always gives a constant
figure. That is to say, if one operator is working hard and does the
job in a very short time, he will be given a high effort rating. When
these are multiplied together they will give a certain figure. Another
operator, working more slowly, will take a longer time on the job.
His effort rating, however, will be lower. When his time and rating
are multiplied together, they will give the same figure as the first
operator. This can be shown in a simple formula:

$$\text{Observed Time} \times \text{Rating} = \text{Constant (K)}$$

Activity Sampling

The most accurate method of work measurement is, of course,
the detailed time study. It is, however, the most expensive, since it
means a trained work study engineer standing over the operator for
fairly long periods. Are there any other methods that will give
adequate results for less expenditure of time and money? Several of
these exist which we shall outline in a moment, but the problem of
accuracy crops up here.

Anything short of a detailed study over a period of time is a
'sample'. But how far can we depend on this 'sample' as a representation of what is being done? Think of the domestic situation
again. You get a chance to pop in during the morning and you find
your wife sitting down having a cup of tea. Does this mean that she
spends all day just idling around? Or is this the only ten minutes
when she's taken the weight off her feet during a busy and tiring
day? You can't possibly know from one single observation. If,
however, you could look in half a dozen times you'd get a better idea
of how she spends the morning. The accuracy of your conclusions
would be linked up with the number of your observations.

This is the whole problem of sampling, and there are ways of calculating the margin of error. Activity Sampling simply means taking a series of observations over a period, and from these building up a picture of a job. Some form of plan should, of course, be laid out beforehand, usually after a pilot study. We shall also need classifications of what the person being observed is doing at the time. A typical set of these is shown below:

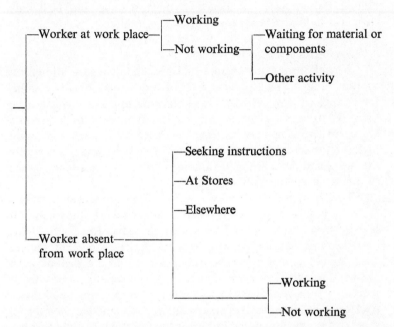

General classifications, however, are of limited usefulness in activity sampling. We want to know in more detail what the operator is actually doing. If he is running a bank of machines, for example, we want to know how many are stopped and why. If he is on a short-cycle, repetitive task, what is holding him up? If it is a long-cycle, non-repetitive task, the observations may not fit exactly into any classification. The number of observations to be taken, the time of each observation, how often and how long, all these need to be planned out beforehand. As a general rule, random observations are more effective than those taken at regular intervals.

There is plenty of room for suspicion and mistrust when activity sampling is used. 'There's that so-and-so spying on us again' can be a typical response when the observer is noticed on the floor. According to the book, this should be dealt with by full consultation beforehand to gain the co-operation of everybody concerned. This sounds fine, and every effort should be made to carry it out in practice. But who is it that deals with all the small day-to-day niggles on the factory floor? Who calms people down when they get a bit agitated? Whose word is trusted when he tells them it's not just another gimmick to get more work for less money? You know the answer to this one already! And the essential point is that the supervisory manager himself should have confidence in the technique. But he'll only trust it if he understands the general idea behind it.

Synthetics and Standards Data

When a work study engineer has been in one organization for a year or so, he'll have looked at a lot of very similar jobs. In a store, for example, there will be a lot of stacking to do. Articles will be lifted off trolleys and placed on shelves. Some may be larger and some smaller; some may be heavy and some light; some may go on high shelves and some on lower ones. The task, however, is basically the same, and these are only variations on it. Isn't it rather a waste of time to study them all separately?

This is where we come up against what are called Synthetic Data. After a bit of time on this sort of job, the work study man can lay down standard times for various elements. He can say, for example, that it takes so long to lift a package one foot square, weighing one pound, from the trolley and lay it on a shelf at waist height. When this job crops up again, he can use this time without making a fresh study. He will have other times for larger and heavier packages, for higher shelves and so on. The more of these 'synthetic' times he has, the fewer studies he will need to make. Sooner or later, in fact, he'll be able to set a time for a job without even seeing it done. He can build it up from the standard times which he's already got for each element.

Predetermined Motion Time Systems (PMTS)

The ideas behind synthetics are the basis for what is called Predetermined Motion Time Systems or PMTS. (This is the British term, though you may come across MTM, or Methods Time Measurement, which is an American term meaning the same thing.) The general idea behind these is that all manual work is made up of different combinations of a small number of basic motions. Standard times for these have been worked out by detailed studies. A number of work study engineers, working quite separately, have built up a large number of observations. These have been computed statistically, and standards agreed on an international basis. Thus, when a new job is planned, the basic motions which make it up can be determined beforehand. The job, in fact, can be seen as a pattern of these pre-determined motions. As we already have the standard times for each of these, we simply add these together to get the time for the job.

The definition is as follows:

Predetermined Motion Time Systems: A work measurement technique whereby times established for basic human motions (classified according to the nature of the motion and the conditions under which it is made) are used to build up the time for a job at a defined level of performance. (BSI 3138, 1959. Glossary of terms in work study.)

Here again we are obviously on specialist ground. PMTS has involved a great deal of detailed study. Its practitioners must undergo special training and must have a mass of information at their command. It is, however, another general idea that the modern supervisory manager must have at his disposal. He may not be equipped to practise it himself. But he should know what those who are so equipped are trying to do.

Network Analysis

Work measurement of individual jobs makes an important contribution to efficiency. But we must be careful not to get too tied down to detail. In certain large and complex projects the overall planning of operations will be quite as important as the individual jobs. This is where the idea of a 'network' of activities becomes important. And the problem now becomes one of organizing these into a sequence of events that can be undertaken in a logical order; and also to deal with situations where more than one event is taking place at the same time. Once again we make use of diagrams to record what is happening, and the symbols are as follows:

A solid arrow represents an 'activity', its head showing the finish and its tail showing the beginning. The length of the arrow does not correspond with the time of the activity, this being inserted in figures. In this kind of diagram it is necessary to adjust the lengths of activity-arrows to show how they fit together.

A 'node', which represents a moment in time, such as when an activity starts or finishes.

------->   A dotted arrow, called a 'dummy'. These are used to show how various activities link up with each other in a network. They have no significance in time, nor do they represent activities in themselves.

To give a simple example of the use of these symbols, let us think of moving a machine from one shop to another. To show this as a network, we would break it down into the following activities and durations (or times):

1 Disconnect machine from services   20 min
2 Move machine to new position   60 min
3 Prepare new position and services   40 min
4 Install machine in new position   50 min
5 Connect with services   20 min
6 Run in and test   50 min

This would be shown on the diagram as follows:

FIG. 13

When we add in the times for each activity cumulatively, we get a total of 240 minutes for the whole operation.

FIG. 14

A closer study of such a diagram, however, might give us the idea that two activities could be carried out at the same time. Once the machine has been disconnected from the services in its existing position, a couple of men could go over to prepare the new position, while the remainder were moving it across. This diagram would then look like this:

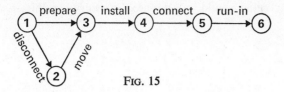

Fig. 15

And the times would work out as follows:

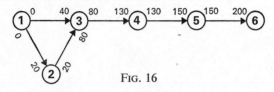

Fig. 16

This very simple illustration should show the general idea behind network analysis. If you think of a large construction project, where all sorts of different activities are going on at the same time, you will see how it can be applied in practice.

Critical Path Analysis

One of the results of network analysis is to show which activities must be completed before others can be started. In the little example above, the machine could not be installed before the new position had been prepared. Nor could it be connected up before it had been installed. In any network there will be a sequence of such activities, which form a kind of central line through it. This is known as the 'critical path', and the starting and finishing times along it determine the timing of the whole network. Critical path analysis begins with a study of these earliest and latest starting times.

Take the following list of activities:

Activity	Duration	Condition
A	1 min	Starts with B and C
B	2 min	Starts with A and C
C	3 min	Starts with A and B
D	4 min	Follows A
E	5 min	Follows B and joins F
F	6 min	Follows C and joins E
G	7 min	Follows D, joins H, but cannot be commenced until E and F have been completed
H	8 min	Follows E and F and joins G

These activities would link up into a network like this:

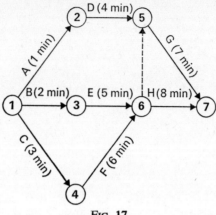

Fig. 17

When we insert the earliest starting times into the network we get the following picture:

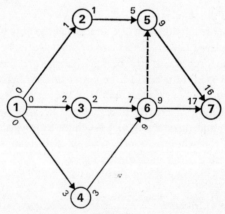

Fig. 18

As G cannot start until E and F have been completed, we have a 4-minute delay at node 5. As H also depends on both E and F, we have another 2-minute delay at node 6. The total time required for the whole network is 17 minutes.

When we redraw the network with the latest starting times, working backwards from a total of 17 minutes, we get the following picture:

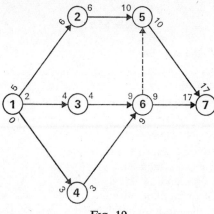

FIG. 19

Comparing these two diagrams, there is one path which has the same times for both earliest and latest starting. This goes along nodes 1, 4, 6, and 7, linking up activities C, F, and H. This is the critical path where there is no 'float' between the earliest and latest starting times. At node 5, for example, there is a float of 4 minutes between activities D and G. At node 6 there is a float of 2 minutes between activities E and H. And at node 7 there is a float of 1 minute between activities G and H. Along the critical path, however, there is no float or room for delay, so that any deviation from these times will upset the overall time for the network.

Civil engineering; assembly work where components are made in different departments or possibly in outside firms; construction work which depends on sub-contracting major items: all these offer scope for critical path analysis. It makes possible the planning of an even flow of work, the cutting down of waiting times, reductions in cost, particularly in the capital tied up in a process. It also provides a means of control, calling attention to any deviations from the critical path which could result in delays or alterations in other parts of the programme. In some parts of the network above, delays can be allowed for, as at nodes 5, 6, and 7. Along the critical path, however, any delay will hold up the whole process.

SUMMARY

1 *What is Work Measurement?*

It is 'the application of techniques designed to establish the time for a qualified operator to carry out a specified task at a defined level of performance'. (BSI 3138, 1959. Glossary of terms in work study.)

2 *What problems does it present?*

    (a) The emotional reaction of the operator.
    (b) Establishing a standard method for the job.
    (c) Setting a standard of skill.
    (d) Setting a standard of effort.
    (e) Making allowance for any other relevant factors.

3 *How do we standardize the Skill Factor?*

By taking an operator of 'average' skill. This raises problems of its own, but with experience it is not difficult to pick out an operator who is neither particularly highly skilled nor especially lacking in skill on the job.

4 *How do we standardize the Effort Factor?*

By using a rating scale based on 'normal' effort—that is, when an operator is working neither especially fast nor especially slowly. There are problems in establishing this scale which can be overcome by careful training of work study specialists.

5 *What is a Relaxation Allowance?*

This is an allowance for fatigue or other forms of stress in a job. A percentage is added to the representative extended or normalized time, to give a standard time for a job.

6 *What is the basic unit in Work Measurement?*

This is the Standard Minute. It represents the amount of work done by an operator of average skill, working at normal effort in one minute by the clock. It can be applied to any form of manual work and consists of Extended Time plus Allowances.

7 *What is Activity Sampling?*

This is a method of collecting samples by spaced observations and classifying what is observed under appropriate headings. It raises the problem of how accurately the samples observed represent the whole job content.

8 *What are Predetermined Motion Time Systems (PMTS)?*

These are 'synthetic data'. 'A work measurement technique whereby times established for basic human motions (classified according to the nature of the motion and the conditions under which it is made) are used to build up the time for a job at a defined level of performance.' (BSI 3138, 1959. Glossary of terms in work study.)

9 *What do we mean by Network Analysis?*

In a large or complex project, the individual operations, with their times, can be recorded on a diagram. This will show up the necessary sequence with the inevitable delays when one operation cannot begin until another is completed. From this a 'critical path' can be worked out, showing the minimum time for the whole operation, and how subsidiary activities must be fitted in.

There are many different ways of paying people for the work they do. In the final analysis, however, they boil down to one or other of two systems. Either you can pay a chap for the time he spends on the premises. Or you can pay him for the results he produces. Any wage payment system is a variation on one or other of these. Each has its advantages and disadvantages, and attempts have been made to get the best of both worlds by a compromise between the two.

The main advantage of the time-rate method of payment is its simplicity. You agree to pay an employee so much an hour, so much a day, a week, a month, or a year. So long as he's been at work for the agreed time, no more records are needed. There may be a slight complication if he's put in some overtime, which you've agreed to pay at an increased rate. This, however, only involves checking up when he arrived and when he left the building. Time-rate payment also lets the employee know where he stands. He can rely on a regular wage or salary for as long as he's in the job. If there's any negotiation about rates of payment, that again is simple and straightforward. Employees can bargain individually or collectively about time rates. No matter how tough the bargaining may be, once these are agreed, payment can be adjusted to the new scale.

The big problem about time-rate payment, however, is how much work does the employee do when he's in the building? If he's a conscientious, hard-working type, he'll put in a decent day's work for his money. But what is a decent day's work? We've discussed some of the complications about this in the chapter on work measurement. If, on the other hand, he's not so conscientious and hard-working, who makes sure that he puts in a day's work? The supervisory manager, of course! And this raises the question of whether *he's* conscientious enough—or tough enough—to see that the people under him do their stint. All of this points up the disadvantages of time-rate payment. They could be summed up as the difficulty of seeing that you get value for money.

Payment by results has the opposite advantages and disadvantages. If you agree to pay so much a piece, then if the chap doesn't produce many pieces, he doesn't get much money. This throws the responsibility on to him for how hard he works. If he wants to earn a decent living, he'll have to produce a lot of pieces. Even the stupidest clot can understand that. This is the main advantage of payment by results, and it is a very real one. Any scheme based on this principle always results in a higher output per man-hour.

There are, however, a lot of problems. Some of these arise from the more complicated administration. Someone has to record what each operator has produced and check that it is up to standard for quality. Some of the problems concern the provision of work, tools, and other items necessary for the job. If there's a hold-up somewhere and he's got to wait around, does this come out of his earnings? He'll take a poor view of that, and he'll either kick up a fuss about being kept short of work—this may be a good thing, for it will put pressure on someone to get things moving again (probably the supervisory manager)—or he'll claim that he ought to be paid for delays that aren't his fault. Here we have a bargaining situation, which is another big problem about payment by results. You've really turned the employee into a sub-contractor, producing work for you at an agreed price. This gives him plenty of opportunities to bargain for a little bit more here and a little bit more there. And if one employee, or a group of employees, manages to strike a good bargain on a new product or a new method, the others will be quick to complain that their earnings are too low. This is the problem of 'wage drift'. It means that earnings are going up faster than output, which, of course, pushes up the wage cost of the product.

Levels of Earnings

On a time-rate method of payment, how is the level of wages or salaries decided? This is a difficult question, for there are all sorts of influences at work. The first and most obvious of these is the number of people looking for jobs. Laws of supply and demand apply here, as they do in every aspect of our economic life. If unemployment is high, wages are low. When unemployment comes down, wage rates go up.

This is true in general terms, but there are ways of beating the market. If a particular skill is scarce, it will command better wages, even in times of unemployment. Similarly if a skill can be made scarce, by those who possess it banding together and bargaining collectively, employers will have to pay more for it. Collective bargaining is one of the functions of trade unions, and it is an essential one. Workers are at a disadvantage in bargaining one at a time with their employer. He can usually do without any one of them longer than that person can do without his wages. In the past, when there was very little welfare provision by the State, this put workers very much at the mercy of the factory owners. By sticking together in the trade unions, they got on more level terms. So nowadays in most industries, national agreements are negotiated between Employers' Federations and Trade Unions, to lay down basic time rates. These are frequently added to by payment-by-results schemes, but we shall leave these for the moment.

Within any one company, however, there will be a mixture of people. Some will be represented by one union, some by another, and some will have no union at all. If we leave wage rates to be settled by those market forces, we shall finish up with a lot of nonsenses. Some people who find themselves in a strong bargaining position, either through the scarcity of their particular skill or through effective union representation, will be doing very well for themselves. Others, whose bargaining position is weak, will be underpaid in relation to their value to the organization. If a situation like this is allowed to continue, it will lead to trouble. And this trouble may not take the obvious line of formal grievances or strikes. It may take the less obvious, but possibly more serious, line of useful employees leaving one at a time for better-paying jobs. And those who remain falling into the 'Well, what's it matter anyhow? There's nothing in it for me' attitude, which undermines the morale of the organization.

Job Evaluation

For its own protection, therefore, an organization should make sure that its 'wage structure' makes sense. Rates for different jobs should be logically related to one another, so that those which make heavier demands and are of more value to the company, carry more money than the simpler, less significant jobs. This is where the technique known as *job evaluation* comes in. Note, however, that up to this point we are concerned with the *relation* of one rate of payment to another, not the actual amounts of money paid. Job evaluation is a technique for comparing the worth of jobs, one with another. These values will later have to be translated into wage rates. When this is done, however, each should bear a sensible relation to the rest.

There are various systems of job evaluation, the simplest of which is the Ranking Method. Each job is printed on a card, and people are asked to arrange them in order. The one considered of most value to the organization is placed first. The next most valuable is placed second, and so on down to the job which seems least important. Several people can be asked to rank the cards, and it is surprising how closely they agree. This method cuts through all the complications. It is sometimes considered too simple, however, for the steps between the various jobs may not always be the same.

Another method is to classify jobs in *groups* or *grades*. These might be, for example, unskilled jobs, semi-skilled, skilled, highly skilled, and so on. This method, again, is simple and easily understood, but problems sometimes arise over the differences between the grades. It might be difficult to be sure whether someone high up in the semi-skilled grade is of less value than someone low down in the skilled grade. We might feel that we need a method which allows finer comparisons to be made.

The answer to this is the Points System of job evaluation. A series of overall requirements which enter into any job is first set up. Various classifications can be used, some of which go into more detail than others. One of the simplest lists the following five:

Mental requirements
Skill requirements
Physical requirements
Responsibility
Working conditions

Points are given under each of these requirements on a scale from, say, 1 to 10. If the job requires a high degree of skill, it would get a value of 8 or 9 under this heading. If it made heavy physical demands, it would get a similarly high value under that heading. When all the points are added together, they give a numerical value for the job.

In most cases this points system gives a useful comparison of one job with another. It can, however, run into trouble. For example, we might have a job with a high mental requirement, such as research and development, carried on in a comfortable office all day long. This might get 9 for mental requirements but only 1 for working conditions. Against this one, we might have someone stacking boxes in a deep freeze—1 for mental requirements and 9 for the very cold working conditions. These values cancel each other out, so two widely different jobs come out equal. This, of course, is an extreme case, but it illustrates what some people consider to be a limitation of the points system.

The way to get over this is to use what is called the Factor Comparison Method. This gives 'weights' to the different requirements in the total value of the job. If, for example, the mental requirements were thought to be more important than the working conditions, their score could be multiplied by 3. This would give it more weight when the figures were added up. This factor comparison method can become a bit complicated and thus may defeat its object.

For if people are going to have any faith in a job evaluation system, they must be able to understand it. There is a lot to be said, therefore, for keeping it as simple as possible.

The general idea of job evaluation should now be fairly clear. We should be able to see a scale of different values on which one job

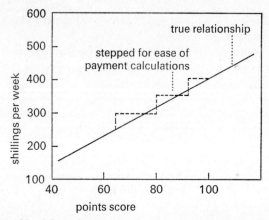

FIG. 20. *Job evaluation graph: points to wages conversion*

is related logically to another. But these have still to be translated into actual wages or salaries. The normal method of doing this is to take one or more fixed points on the scale. And to set a money value on these in terms of the going rates of weekly or monthly earnings. We could say, for example, that a skilled job, with a points value of 100, should carry 400 shillings or £20 a week. Any job with a higher value than this would carry more money. Those with a lower value would carry less. The graph shown in Fig. 20 illustrates how these values can be translated into money terms.

Merit Rating

Once a wage or salary structure has been set up and is working satisfactorily, it can become a bit rigid. True, it may be moved up as the general level of earnings rises, and any organization should be on the watch for this. Various figures are published by the Ministry of Labour and other bodies which show how earnings are moving. There is also a Cost-of-Living Index, or an Index of Retail Prices, which has been going up steadily for the past few years. But any changes made for these reasons will be changes in the structure as a whole. They may not mean much to the chap who's been slogging away at the same point on the salary scale since as long as he can remember. Once again what's in it for him? Similar considerations apply to people whose jobs cannot be related to a payment-by-results scheme—administrative and clerical staff.

This can be dealt with by what is called Merit Rating. At each point in the scale some variation can be allowed for. Instead of laying down exactly £20 for a skilled man, we can leave a margin between £18 and £22. When a chap is appointed to the job, he can start at the lower limit of £18. If, after a period, he is reported on as a satisfactory employee, he can be moved up to the mid-point of £20. If he is reported later as performing exceptionally well, he can be moved up to the top limit of £22. This provides a certain incentive to the efficient worker, but it does raise other problems. Who does the reporting, and what standard does he use? It is not unusual to find, after a few years, that every man in the section has been pushed up to the top rate. This would mean that they are all above average, which sounds rather odd. What has happened, of course, is that no one has had the guts to put in a bad report on anyone.

Payment by Results

Piecework has a long history. For many years miners have been paid so much a ton for coal at the pithead; navvies so much a ton for earth moved; weavers so much a yard for cloth woven. Piece prices were fixed by bargaining between the workers or their ganger on the one hand, and the boss on the other. When they worked hard and the job went well, they earned good money. When things didn't go so well, their earnings suffered. This method of payment, primitive though it may have been, provided a simple and effective incentive for the worker to put his back into the job and get out the production.

The piecework attitude of mind has not yet died out in industry. In many places, work study men are still referred to as 'rate fixers' and regarded as people with whom to bargain over the rate for the job. If you can do them down and fiddle the piecework prices, you've scored over the management. If, on the other hand, they manage to outsmart you and fix a tight rate, they've won that round. Never mind; with a bit of luck you'll probably win the next one. No one in contact with the factory floor can ignore this way of looking at things. In some way it is a healthy attitude, for conflict can be constructive. It keeps people on their toes and adds a bit of zip to the task of earning your living. It does, however, run against the general ideas we have been discussing.

In the preceding chapter we have been considering how work can be studied systematically and objectively. This should take us out of the world of hunch and guesswork; away from the 'We've always done it that way' and 'I reckon it takes about so long' kind of thinking. We should now be able to lay down standards of work, and pay an agreed price for these standards. A satisfactory payment-by-results scheme depends on the following steps:

1 A defined method of working, built up from a properly conducted method study.
2 An agreed level of output at standard performance. This will be got by work measurement on the methods described. It will be expressed in so many standard minutes for each piece or operation.
3 An agreed relationship between the increase in output and a rise in earnings. This, like the point above, will have to be negotiated with worker representatives. (It is always possible that these negotiations may arouse more interest on the factory floor than the TUC's annual conference!)

To illustrate how this works in practice, let us consider an operator working on a job that has a value of 20 standard minutes per 100 pieces. We shall take this as the work-measurement standard on the lines already set out. He is working an 8-hour day and he produces 2,400 pieces. His performance is calculated as follows:
2,400 pieces at 20 standard minutes per 100=480 standard minutes
He has worked 8 hours by the clock   =480 clock minutes

He has therefore produced the same number of standard minutes as he has worked minutes by the clock. We can thus express his performance as a percentage like this:

$$\frac{480 \text{ standard minutes}}{480 \text{ minutes by the clock}} \times 100 = 100\%$$

Suppose, however, he has only produced 2,160 pieces in the 8-hour day. This would work out as:

$$\frac{432 \text{ standard minutes}}{480 \text{ minutes by the clock}} \times 100 = 90\%$$

Suppose, on the other hand, he has produced 2,640 pieces in the 8-hour day. This would give us:

$$\frac{528 \text{ standard minutes}}{480 \text{ minutes by the clock}} \times 100 = 110\%$$

A payment-by-results scheme can thus be based upon work measurement. This, in fact, is the proper way to operate such schemes. It has certain advantages. One of these is that various different jobs can be measured in the same terms, in standard minutes. At the end of the day, no matter what he may have been working on, the operator's performance can be added up in these units. Moreover, these units are not mere guesses. They are all measures, made by the same methods and comparable with one another. If, for any reason, the operator has been prevented from working by circumstances beyond his control, allowance can be made for this.

The operator's overall performance can now be summed up in the following terms:

$$\frac{\text{Total standard minutes of work produced}}{\text{Attendance time}-(\text{authorized waiting time}+\text{diverted time}+\text{any unmeasured work})}$$

This formula can be used universally. It can not only measure an operator's efficiency, but can also be used for a group, a section, a department, or a whole factory.

Rates for Increased Efficiency

Have we now taken the bargaining out of payment-by-results? By no means. We may have worked out more accurate units of work in our standard minutes. We may have included in these a Relaxation Allowance. We may have set aside waiting time and other interruptions beyond the operator's control. And we may have expressed his working efficiency as a percentage. But we have not yet decided what we are going to pay for this increased efficiency. This must still be agreed through the normal process of negotiation.

We should, however, be clear about what we are bargaining over. This is the relationship between increased efficiency and payment. The following graph (Fig. 21) should make this clear. It shows a direct relationship between the two. A $33\frac{1}{3}\%$ increase in efficiency results in a $33\frac{1}{3}\%$ increase in payment.

When we come to look at a payment-by-results scheme in a particular factory, however, it may not be quite so simple as this. There will usually be a minimum level, below which earnings are not allowed to fall for 'policy reasons'. This is a phrase which covers a multitude of sins. What it means in this case is a weekly pick-up below which you can't get anyone to work. This 'timework rate' will be made up of the negotiated rate, plus a national award, plus a

cost-of-living bonus, and so on. This is the rate that will be paid to
the operator no matter what his performance may be.

What we have to consider is where and how the increased
earnings (or bonus) start on top of the timework rate. We might
agree that this should be set at 75% efficiency in the terms described
above. Up to this level, the operator would receive his timework rate.
As soon as he goes above it, he would receive an additional payment
related to his increased efficiency. This is illustrated in Fig. 22. We
might note here in passing that the percentage efficiency is often

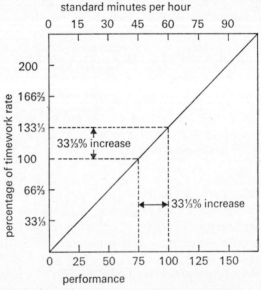

FIG. 21. *The straight proportional performance/payment relationship*

referred to as 'performance'. Thus, if you hear anyone talking about
a '75 performance' or a '100 performance' this is what he means.

Having decided the point at which bonus or increased earnings
start—in this case a 75 performance—we now have to agree on how
these are to be related to increased efficiency. In many cases 133⅓%
of the timework rate is paid for a 100 performance. This again is
illustrated in the diagram. If performance increases above the 100
level, bonus will continue to rise in the same proportion. This is
known as the 75–100 straight proportional scheme.

We hope that by now the general idea of relating earnings to
performance will be clear. It is important to stick to these general
ideas, for payment-by-results schemes can become very complicated
—so complicated, in fact, that one wonders whether the people con-

cerned really understand them. To keep things clear, we shall list some of the complications.

1 Unmeasured work. If an operator has to spend time on jobs that have not been measured and a bonus set, he will be paid for this at timework rate. There are sometimes protests about this, and as a result of negotiations, average earnings may be paid.

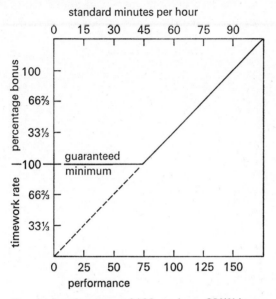

Standard performance of 100 produces 33⅓% bonus

Fig. 22. *75–100 (straight proportional) payment scheme*

2 Varying work content. However accurate the work measurement may be, there is always the possibility that the work content may not remain exactly standard. An example of this might be the fettling of castings. One batch might have more surplus metal on than another, so that although the operator works at the same effort, his output might vary from batch to batch. His earnings would then move up and down for reasons beyond his control. This is dealt with by rotating the bonus line around the 100-performance/33⅓% bonus point as in Fig. 23. This is known as 'gearing'. The effect of this is that when his performance falls below 100, the operator does not lose all his bonus. While, when it goes above 100, he does not gain quite so much. The illustration shown is known as the 50–100 operator scheme.

3 Bedaux, Rowan, and Halsey Schemes. On a straight piecework basis, over and above guaranteed minimum earnings, the further the operator goes above the 100 performance, the more bonus he earns. This can raise problems, and some payment-by-results schemes provide for a lower rate of bonus above this level. Without going into detail, three typical schemes are illustrated in Fig. 24.

4 Multi-factor schemes. It may be advisable in certain cases to take other factors into account, over and above the effort of the operator. One of these may be scrap or quality of work. Fig. 25 shows

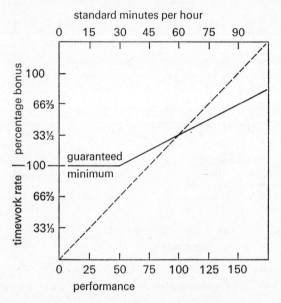

Standard performance of 100 produces 33⅓% bonus

FIG. 23. *50–100 operator payment scheme*

how this can be dealt with in calculating bonus. Great care should be taken in designing schemes of this type as they can easily get out of hand. It is advisable to try them out on the previous year's figures to see how the operator's earnings would have been affected. This usually helps when it comes to getting the scheme accepted.

5 General considerations. As we pointed out above, money is always a hot subject. And anything that will affect a worker's earnings can give rise to strong feelings. Payment-by-results schemes will always be subject to bargaining, and when this gets down to detail it can result in some funny little things being written in. Workers and their representatives are not stupid. And one sometimes feels that they can run rings round the work study man. The following points should therefore be borne in mind when designing a bonus scheme.

(a) It should be simple enough for the operator to calculate his earnings from the output he has produced.
(b) Bonus earned in one period should not affect that in any other period.

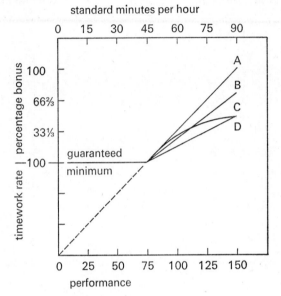

FIG. 24. *Incentive scheme comparisons*

(c) There should be as short a time as possible between the operator earning his bonus and his being notified of the results.
(d) The operator should be paid for his own work only, whenever possible. Where group schemes are in use, the group should be kept small, so that the effect of individual members' effort can be seen and understood. As soon as the group becomes too large, the effect on individual incentive is lost.

Measured Daywork
Payment-by-results schemes can become very complicated, as

we have said. They involve a great deal of recording of standard minutes produced, waiting time, and so on. They require a lot of calculation to find out what the chap has actually earned. This is non-productive work, and there is something to be said for trying to get rid of it. This has led to the scheme known as Measured Daywork.

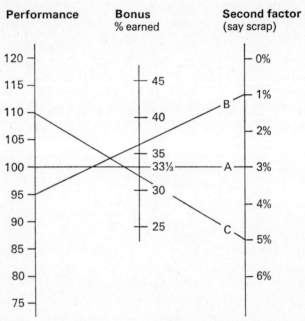

A Operator with 100 performance and 3% scrap receives 33⅓% bonus
B Operator with 95 performance and 1% scrap receives 36% bonus
C Operator with 110 performance and 5% scrap receives 32% bonus

FIG. 25. *Multi-factor incentive scheme—two factors*

The general idea behind this is to pay a high time rate, and to set a standard of efficiency for each job. So long as the operator meets this standard, he gets the high hourly rate. If he fails to meet that standard, he is transferred to another job. Allowance is made, of course, for circumstances beyond his control, for time to learn the job, pick up speed, and so on. But basically his fixed earnings depend on meeting the standards set. Work measurement has been used, of course, to set these standards.

To some extent, measured daywork makes the most effective use of the methods we have been describing. It makes possible the setting of standards for efficient performance. And in a factory where one process depends on another, the whole production plan can be laid out on these standards. It makes possible the efficient use of labour, for if these standards are being met, the wage cost of the product is being kept within bounds. It makes high earnings possible, and we must never forget that people come to work to earn a living. But it puts a lot of responsibility on the supervisory manager. He comes back into the picture as the man to whom the operator is directly responsible.

Payment-by-results schemes have the effect of making the work situation impersonal. The chap comes in to earn his money. If he produces the output he gets it. If he plays around and chats to his mates, his earnings fall off. But that's up to him, isn't it? And if the supervisor tries to tell him off for idling around, he can always reply, 'Well, what about it? It's my pocket that's suffering, isn't it? What are you worrying about? You mind your own business and I'll mind mine.' This has the result of lowering the supervisor's influence on the floor. It turns him into a kind of service hand who sees to the flow of material and keeps the equipment running. Measured daywork puts him back into the centre of things as the man in charge. It requires a more direct and personal relationship between him and his operators. He's got to help them meet the standards of the job. And if they can't do so, he's got to decide about moving them to another one. Or, in the last resort, getting them shifted out of the section.

Productivity Bargaining

Two pressures are always at work in production industry. One is for lower costs, and the other for higher earnings. The only way these can be reconciled is by improving the efficiency of labour utilization. Effective work study is the way to achieve this. There is no reason why an operator should not take home forty pounds a week without affecting the labour cost of the product. Provided, of course, that his time and effort is being properly applied.

Productivity bargaining is appearing more and more often in the news nowadays. The first case to hit the headlines was at the Esso refinery at Fawley, where they cut down overtime while at the same time keeping earnings up to the former figure. This was done by the better use of labour through systematic studies of work. Supervisory managers should be prepared for this sort of thing happening in their own organization. So long as they understand the general ideas behind them they should be able to cope with the changes. And always remember that they are the people who've got to make them work in practice.

Profit Sharing

As we mentioned above, piecework turns the individual operator into a sub-contractor. He's only concerned with his own earnings, and he doesn't worry much about how his job fits into the work of the organization. If he can work a little fiddle to push his money up, he'll do so. It doesn't bother him if this upsets the smooth flow of production through the section. Or even if it makes someone else's job more difficult.

To avoid all this, schemes have been devised to make the individual's payment depend on the overall efficiency of the organization. The simplest of these is Profit Sharing. A proportion of the firm's profit for the year is set aside for the personnel. This is paid out as a bonus, usually in the form of a percentage on earnings. In some cases it can be turned into Workers' Shares, on which dividends are paid in the same way as to other shareholders in the company. The general idea is that workers will thus have an interest in the overall efficiency of the organization, and not merely in their own immediate earnings.

There are variations in the general idea of profit sharing. One of these is the Scanlon Plan, which has been popular in the United States. One or two companies have experimented with it over here also. The overall intention remains the same, however—to relate individual earnings to overall efficiency. One of the difficulties arises from the size of the organization. In a small company, it is usually easy for the individual operator to understand what is going on. He knows when the place is doing well, and if the boss whacks out a bit of a bonus at Christmas, he'll feel that this is his share of the profits. This is fair enough, he'll think, and he'll do his best to help in making the little company successful next year. But in a large organization, there's a big gap between the operator's day-to-day job and the financial results at the end of the year. And if these results are published, they're usually in very large figures indeed. It doesn't seem to make all that difference if he works a bit harder today, or saves a few shillings' worth of material. This'll never be noticed against all those thousands of pounds. So he might as well take it easy and not mind about the odd bits of scrap. This harks back to the point we made above about keeping the time between work and earnings as short as possible.

Profit-sharing schemes have rather a mixed history. In some

cases they have been successful. In others they haven't come up to expectations. It is always a mistake to think that one gimmick will make all the difference to a firm's efficiency. There are a lot of factors, each of which plays its part—organization, planning, methods, and control. But the most important of the lot is day-to-day supervision on the job.

SUMMARY

1 *What are the advantages and disadvantages of the time-rate method of payment?*

Its main advantage is its simplicity. Payment by the hour, day, week, or year requires little recording or calculation. Its disadvantage lies in the difficulty of controlling the amount of work done in the time paid for.

2 *What are the advantages and disadvantages of payment-by-results?*

Its main advantage lies in relating payment to the productive effort of the individual. It has the disadvantage of requiring more complicated administration and providing scope for bargaining on details which, in a time of full employment, can lead to wage drift.

3 *What determines the level of earnings at work?*

Several influences affect this, mainly arising from market factors. The level of employment, the scarcity of certain types of skill, the bargaining advantages of trade unions; all these can play a part in making an organization's wage or salary structure illogical and unfair.

4 *What do we mean by Job Evaluation?*

Job evaluation is a means of working out the relative value of jobs in a logical manner. It can be done by the Ranking Method, by classifying jobs in grades, by the Points System of allocating numerical values to a series of job requirements, or by the Factor Comparison Method. The values thus arrived at can be translated into money terms, usually by taking one or more fixed points on the evaluation scale, and expressing these in current earnings.

5 *What do we mean by Merit Rating?*

In a wage or salary structure, margins can be left at each level. Employees' earnings can be moved up and down within these margins according to reports on their performance on the job.

6 *How should a payment-by-results scheme be planned?*

Agreed levels of output for each operation should be set in standard minutes by means of work measurement. The operator's efficiency can then be calculated as a percentage of standard minutes against minutes by the clock. Efficiency measured in these terms can then be related to payment.

7 *What do we mean by Measured Daywork?*

Measured daywork means the setting up of efficiency standards for each job and the payment of a high time rate. To earn this rate, the operator must keep to these efficiency standards. This throws added responsibility on the supervisory manager instead of, as in payment-by-results, leaving the responsibility for output on the operator.

8 *What do we mean by Productivity Bargaining?*

This is a general term covering agreements to relate earnings to efficiency. It can take many forms, but its applications depend on having a reliable measure of working efficiency.

9 *What is the point of Profit Sharing?*

It is an attempt to relate the operator's earnings to the overall efficiency of the company, rather than to his immediate job. In some cases, particularly in small organizations, this can be effective. In large organizations, the gap between his immediate task and the yearly financial results is too wide for him to see the relationship.

New products start off in the design department. They are worked out to meet customers' requirements, either one at a time or for a mass market. Specifications are made out and standards are set. The product is then complete, either as an idea in the designer's mind or as a prototype. The designer has now done his job. It is up to the production people to make the product to the standards set by the designer. And this is where the headaches begin!

In this chapter we shall be concerned with meeting these standards. In some cases they may be difficult to reach with production plant working on large quantities. In other cases they may be more rigid than is actually necessary. Discussions and negotiations may therefore be started to reach modifications acceptable to both parties. The result of these will be a set of standards which the designer agrees are adequate, and which the production people accept as being possible to achieve in practice. These modified standards, however, must be strictly adhered to throughout the production process. And this is where the Quality Control or Inspection System takes over.

Quality Control means inspection, for the only way we can make sure that products are up to standard is by checking them. This immediately raises a number of questions.

Who does the checking?
How does he do it?
When does he do it?
Does he know what he is looking for?
Can he recognize it when he sees it?
What happens when he finds that the product is not up to standard?

If we deal with these questions in turn, we should end up with a general understanding of what quality control is all about.

1 Who does the inspection?

When a skilled man is working in a jobbing shop, he probably does a good deal of his own inspection. That is to say, when he has finished a job, he checks it over to see that it matches up with the specification, which will usually be on a drawing. The supervisory manager may occasionally look over it with him, or he may call the supervisor in if he is in doubt about anything. There is a certain rather expensive motor-car where the production process is accompanied by a log-book for each vehicle. As the skilled tradesman completes his job on the car, on the suspension, the transmission, the engine, and so on, he makes a note in the log-book and signs it. This is the foundation on which the reputation of these cars for high quality is based. The only pity is that people like us can't afford them.

Semi-skilled workers can also do their own inspecting, but here the situation is rather different. The skilled man knows what to look for, and he's generally got enough pride in his trade for his checking-up to be done conscientiously. The semi-skilled man may not know what to look for, and with his limited knowledge he may not recognize the importance of certain details. We must therefore devise a means of checking that is simple enough for him to use, while at the same time it makes certain that nothing below standard slips through. There are various methods for doing this, the simplest of which is perhaps the 'Go'–'No-Go' pair of gauges. The larger of these is set to the maximum tolerance, say 2·01 inches. The smaller is set to the minimum tolerance, say 1·99 inches. If the part will go into one, but will not go into the other, then it must be between 1·99 and 2·01 inches. That is to say, it is no more than ten thousandths of an inch away from exactly two inches in size.

We may be taking a risk, however, if we leave the responsibility for inspection in the hands of the operator. He may not be quite so conscientious as we would like, especially if he's on piecework. We may decide therefore that we need a specialist, someone from the inspection or quality control department. This is the point where trouble can start, for the supervisory manager may feel that he is no longer king in his own castle. Someone else has been introduced into his section who is directly responsible not to him but to the chief inspector in the front office. This person can make decisions—'I'm not passing that lot'—which the supervisory manager must accept. These decisions can interfere with the smooth working of the section, for products may have to be worked over again or even scrapped. There is room for a lot of argument and bad feeling, if the supervisory manager and the inspector keep getting across each other. It is all very well saying that each must recognize the other's responsibility and respect it, but this is a bit too simple. The supervisory manager has got another functional specialist attached to him, who has taken over what was originally part of his job. In some ways this should make his job easier, but in other ways it raises complications. He will have to live with these complications, however, for there are going to be more and more functional specialists.

How does this inspector go about his job? There are several ways, one of which is to act as a 'patrol inspector'. This is the usual method in a machine shop where the inspector patrols round and picks up pieces at random. He checks these for dimensions, quality, or whatever may be appropriate. If they are up to standard, he moves on to the next machine. If they are not up to standard, he may stop the machine, go through the batch to determine what is wrong, then have the machine reset to the correct tolerances. If a patrol inspector is on the ball, he will usually be there when a machine starts up after a new setting. He will check the first few off, and if they are OK, he will let the operator go ahead.

There is a complication here which we shall go into when we come to discuss simple statistics. How many should the inspector check out of a batch to make sure they are all up to standard? If he wants to be absolutely sure, he must check every one, and in some types of product such a 100% check is carried out. But this will take a lot of time, and, as we know, time costs money. So would it be good enough if he checked every other piece? Or every fifth one? Or simply one in twenty? Or one in a hundred? If he checked only a small sample like one in a hundred, he might happen on the only one that was perfect out of a bad batch. Or the only bad one in a perfect batch. This is the problem of 'sampling' which we shall deal with later on as a statistical problem. In practice, however, a knowledgeable patrol inspector can usually keep control of quality by dipping into each batch and checking a small random sample.

The alternative to a patrol inspection is to choose a point on the production flow where defects can be spotted. Once again, the motorcar final assembly line illustrates this. There are several points on this where an inspector can operate the switches and controls and check the fitting of various components. In other types of production similar inspection points can be set up. Food products are now being made on flow lines, and at various points, samples can be taken out for analysis. This raises the next question.

2 How does the inspector make his check?

This, of course, will depend on the product and the method of production. There will, however, always be a critical factor which will determine whether or not quality is being maintained. In a number of engineering products, this will simply be dimension or size. Accurate measurements can be taken, either by a micrometer, or if the quantities justify them, by pre-set gauges. If a part conforms to these measurements, it is up to standard. If it does not, then it is below standard.

Where parts have to be assembled into a mechanism, the method of inspection may become a little more complex. It is, however, possible to rig up a device by which these mechanisms can be tried out to the standard required. This is often applied to electrical products, where the circuits can be connected up and lights or dial readings used to show whether the current is flowing as it should. Checks with air pressure can be used with pneumatic equipment, or with water pressure for hydraulics. Each type of product presents its own problems, so we cannot attempt to go into detail. The reader should think of his own industry to see if he can find examples of what is being done, or what could be done.

Perhaps one of the most difficult inspection problems arises when 'quality' depends on a number of factors, some of which are difficult to measure. 'Finish' often determines the quality of a product, but can we always be sure just exactly what 'finish' means? It may be the smoothness of the surface, the neatness of the fittings, the colour, or even simply the cleanliness. An experienced person can sum all these up at a glance and make decisions which do not vary much from one to another. But an inexperienced person may find it more difficult to maintain a regular standard of quality.

This is where a more careful specification becomes necessary. An interesting example arose in the grading of tobacco leaves. This used to be considered a highly skilled task, which could only be done by tobacco-graders with many years of experience. In fact, it was generally assumed in that part of the world, that unless your grandfather had been a tobacco-grader, you could never be much use at the job. One organization was faced by a shortage of graders, and before the crop was harvested they called in an expert to study the question. This expert found that the grading of a tobacco leaf depended on a few simple things: its size, its texture, its moisture content, and so on. He trained the labourers who cut the leaves to recognize these and to do their own grading. And that year, the customers said they'd never had a better-graded crop of tobacco.

The whole problem is the setting out of the specification. This is first of all a question for the designer, who must lay down the standards to which the product must conform. These must be broken down into detail for each stage in the production process. Difficulties can crop up here, for the designer usually has the perfect product in mind. He may thus set standards which may be possible on a one-off prototype, but which are too high for flow production plant. Similarly he might set an accurate standard for a part, whereas, in reality, a certain tolerance would work just as well. Practical experience with flow production machinery sometimes results in a modification of standards, without any danger to the final product. The 'engineering' of a design for quantity production into a suitable production process is the responsibility of the planning engineers. They often have to negotiate concessions from the designer.

This again is a case where the supervisory manager can give useful advice. He may find that the standards set are very difficult to achieve in practice, and that the inspectors are finding a high proportion of faults. This will result in a lot of scrap, which costs money. In such a case, it may be possible to widen the tolerances without damage to the quality of the finished product. This does not mean that he should be trying to get away with shoddy workmanship. We must, however, be realistic if we are going to make a production plant a paying proposition. And if a hundredth of an inch tolerance makes no real difference, there is no point in trying to work to an accuracy of a thousandth.

3 When does the inspector make his checks?

The basic principle here is that the check should be made at the earliest possible moment before the scrap starts piling up. Thus, if a machine tool has been set up to produce a run of a thousand parts, the inspector should be on hand to check the first few off. Then, if there is anything not up to standard, it can be put right at once. On the other hand, if the operator has produced a couple of hundred before the fault is detected, we have wasted a lot of material. Similarly, if a complex assembly is found to be faulty because one of the first components doesn't work, we have the same sort of nonsense on our hands.

How the checks should be planned will depend on the production process. We cannot go into detail, for what applies to one would not apply to another. We can only state a general idea and leave it to the individual to apply it in particular cases. If the supervisory manager grasps this general idea, however, he will very quickly recognize the points at which checks should be made in the section of which he is in charge.

A Quality Control Chart can be useful in indicating when checks should be made. This is a method of showing how far products are varying from the standard as time goes on. Suppose we are producing parts which should measure 2 inches across. We lay this out as a horizontal line on the chart. We lay out two other lines above

Component description and number
Details of machine

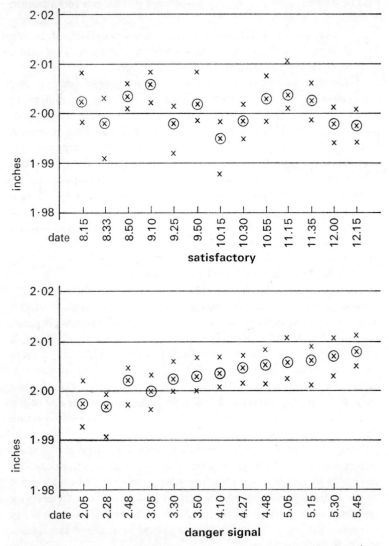

⊗ represents average of sample check; largest and smallest size plotted
above and below the average

FIG. 26. *Control chart*

and below, at 2·01 inches and 1·99 inches. These represent the tolerances which can be accepted, plus or minus ten thousandths of an inch. Then we plot the samples as they are checked. If they are mostly within these lines on the chart, with only the odd one outside as in Fig. 26, then adequate quality is being maintained. But if a tendency appears for a number to be getting near the limit of tolerance, or if a proportion are coming well outside the limit, then something should be done at once. The machine should be stopped and the tool checked for wear, or whatever else may be wrong.

4 Does he know what he is looking for?

When we are dealing with fully trained and experienced inspectors, this raises no problem. They can read the drawings, understand the tolerances, use micrometers and other tools of their trade. Their judgment will be backed by years of experience, and this will also help them to spot things going wrong in the early stages. But they will be expensive, for in the present-day engineering industry, men like these can command good wages. Their use on routine inspection work in a flow production process, therefore, may not be justified. It may be more economical to train someone with less experience to carry out routine checks on the product.

In some factories you can see girls checking parts with pre-set gauges, passing those which fit and rejecting those which don't. You see them dabbing terminals on to various bits of electrical assemblies, and, if the pointer goes up to the right place on the dial, stamping them as up to standard. Inspectors like these have their place in a flow production process, but their experience and judgment may be very limited. The whole point is, of course, that experience and judgment are not called for. By the use of work study techniques the task has been simplified. They are presented with information which is easy to interpret. And the decisions they have to make are of the simplest 'Yes-No' nature.

Before this type of inspector can be effective, however, a great deal of thought and planning must be done. In the first place, the point at which the check is made—the 'When does he do it?' point —must have been decided. This brings up the question discussed above, of cutting down the chances of scrap piling up. Then the measurements or other checks have to be made as simple as possible, so that the information on which the decision is made can be understood at a glance. Then the decision itself must become a simple 'Yes-No' one, without calling for any judgment on the part of the inspector.

Semi-skilled inspectors like these have their limitations. And the supervisory manager must recognize these if he is not going to run into trouble with the Chief Inspector. Although they may be working in a production department and doing a highly simplified job, they are still functional specialists. This means that they are still responsible to the head of that specialist function, in this case the Chief Inspector. It may be that he will decide that it is wise to keep a check on them, so that a senior inspector will look in on them occasionally. Thus we now have an 'inspector of inspectors', which may seem to complicate things a little more. However, if we keep our ideas clear, we shall see how this is justified.

5 Can the inspector recognize what he's looking for when he sees it?

Quite a lot of the points under this heading have already been dealt with. It should now be clear that properly designed check-points should show up faults in a form in which they can be easily recognized. There may always be the case, however, where the inspector scratches his head and says, 'I'm sure there's something wrong here, but I'm blowed if I know what it is.' Such cases should become increasingly uncommon, but as nothing is perfect in human affairs, they will never disappear entirely.

The problem, of course, is to make the standards as objective as possible and to reduce the area of uncertainty. This may not always be as easy as it looks, as has been shown by some studies of inspectors. The same batch of components has been checked separately by two inspectors, each without the knowledge of the other. If the standards were completely objective and properly applied, both inspectors would reject the same number of components and they would both reject the same ones. This has not always proved to be the case, however, and considerable variations in the numbers rejected by different inspectors have been found. A subjective or 'personal opinion' element has thus crept into their judgment.

This is one of the points where we bump up against the conflict between the traditional outlook in the engineering industry and the modern attitude. 'I've been on this job for forty years, and there's nothing I don't know about it. If I say something's right, then it's right, and I'm not standing for any argument.' This kind of person can become more and more of a problem in a modern organization. For, no matter how valuable his experience may be, with advancing technology there are going to be more and more developments that he doesn't know about. To protect his self-esteem, however, he's going to dismiss them as 'new-fangled notions', cling to his traditional knowledge, and fall more and more behind the times. This may be particularly true in inspection or quality control where rule-of-thumb measurements are replaced by micrometers, X-rays, etc.

To keep up with these, an entirely different kind of outlook is necessary—remembering the time when we used to measure in sixteenths of an inch, which seems right out of date now. Then they brought in micrometers and we had to think in thousandths. Now we're beginning to consider thousandths a bit loose. The next thing will be the decimal system and we'll be on to finer tolerances still. Never mind; whatever turns up, you should still be able to cope with it. For, after all, they're only measurements, and no matter how they refine the instruments, they're only applying principles which you can understand as well as anyone else.

6 What happens when the inspector finds that the product is not up to standard?

From the purely quality control point of view, this is where the inspector's job finishes. He's there to check standards, and if he rejects a product it's up to someone else to decide what's to be done about it. Strictly speaking, this is where the supervisory manager takes over, although things may not always be quite so simple.

When anything has been rejected on inspection, two questions arise. First, 'Is it so defective that it must be scrapped?' If so, it represents not only wasted material, but also wasted labour, machine time, and so on. All of these cost money, and in some cases quite a lot of money. So this leads immediately to the second question: 'Is there anything we can do to reclaim it or put it right?' Here again the answer must depend on the type of defect, the product, and the production process. And also on the relative cost of putting it right. If this outweighs the original cost, it is not worth doing. But if there is any way in which the product could be reclaimed without additional cost, this will be the obvious thing to do. Here again, the supervisory manager may produce the idea which saves the company money.

Value Analysis

Quality control and design must link up together, as we have said. Standards necessary to keep up the quality of the product must be adapted to what can be maintained in day-to-day production. Too high standards can add to the cost of the product, while a high proportion of rejects means wasted labour and materials.

This relationship between cost and value can be taken a step further. Each component and each step in the production process represents a cost. But each also makes a contribution to the value of the finished product. *Value analysis* is the study of how much each item of cost contributes to that final value. Its aim is to find how to obtain the maximum value with the minimum cost.

Value analysis is an exercise in teamwork. It starts with a team leader, usually an engineer, and includes someone from the design department, a buyer, a cost accountant, and a production engineer. Other members may be co-opted from work study, O and M, electrical or mechanical engineering specialists, and from supervisory management. Each of these should be a senior man in his own department, coming together for value analysis team meetings. It is essential that they keep in touch with what is going on in their own departments as well as meeting the team leader periodically. The task of the team is to look at various projects, either as recommended by management or on their own initiative. The normal procedure can be broken down into five stages:

1 Information. All known facts about the product are gathered together—drawings, specifications, process layouts, quantities, material supply, and costs. These are considered by the value analysis team in order to find out what each part actually contributes to the finished product.

2 Speculation. This is the stage where as many ideas as possible are generated. It could be compared to a 'brainstorming' session, where every suggestion is welcomed without considering how far it might be practicable. Everyone who might have an idea comes into this stage: outsiders, suppliers of bought-out parts, customers' purchasing units, etc.

3 Investigation. Now the ideas are analysed in order to find those which will work in practice and save money. Those which do not stand up to this test are scrapped; doubtful ones are tested further.

4 Recommendation. By now a formal report can be drawn up showing the savings which can be achieved. This report is sent to every department which is concerned with any stage of the product.

5 Implementation. This is the stage where the supervisory manager comes into the centre of the picture. For while the value analysis team can make recommendations, it is the supervisor who can put them into practice.

Full consultation is essential with everyone concerned in any value analysis exercise, particularly with trade unions and supervision. Where people have been involved in the investigation stage, they will be more likely to co-operate in the implementation stage.

Some companies make use of questionnaires, check-lists, and guide-sheets for purposes of value analysis. Supervisory managers should be ready to take a full part in any value analysis team project when it is presented to them.

SUMMARY

1 *What is the purpose of a Quality Control Department?*

A quality control department has been set up to ensure that all products are up to the standard laid down in the original design. The method by which this purpose is achieved is to arrange for a series of check-points where products can be compared against the specification. This is the process which is commonly called 'inspection'.

2 *How far should quality control be a separate specialist function?*

There may be cases where highly skilled and responsible operators can be left to do their own checking. These, however, are comparatively uncommon. It is more usual to have a specialist inspector attached to each production section, but responsible to a Chief Inspector or Quality Controller. This inspector may patrol the section, making random checks on the products. Or he may remain at a fixed point on the production process, checking each product as it passes that point.

3 *What proportion of products should an inspector check?*

This depends on several things. If the product is an expensive one where a minor variation can render it useless, then each product should be inspected in detail. This is the '100% sample'. If, on the other hand, small variations make no difference, then a small sample can be taken. There are various methods, described in Chapter 9, which can indicate the relation between the size of the sample and the chances of error.

4 *How does the inspector decide whether a product is up to standard?*

In any product there will always be a number of critical factors that determine its quality. These may be dimension, fitting, mechanical accuracy, electrical conductivity, decorative finish or others, depending on the product. These can be stated in quantitative measurements which the inspector can apply. There may be cases where it is difficult to express the factors on which quality depends in terms of measurement. A little ingenuity, however, can usually translate these into objective terms. It is important that the standards should be realistic and capable of being maintained in the productive process.

5 *When should the inspector make his checks?*

At the earliest possible moment to prevent piling up scrap. This will usually be at the beginning of a production run on a machine; or at points in an assembly line where faults can be detected before components are put together in the final product. In addition to these, it is usually good practice for products to be completely checked over before they are delivered to the customer.

6 *What is a Quality Control Chart?*

This is a method of setting out the standard to which a product must conform in horizontal lines on a sheet of paper. As each product is inspected, its measurements can be inserted in the appropriate space. If there is a variation in quality, this will show as a drift away from the standard line. The process can then be checked before this drift begins to exceed the permitted tolerance.

7 *Must the inspector always be a highly trained and experienced man?*

Only if this is justified on economic grounds, in terms of his wages against the costs of faulty products. In many routine inspection jobs, inspectors of limited training and experience can do a perfectly adequate job. In these cases, however, the standards required and the methods of checking must be reduced to very simple terms. The area of personal judgment must be kept to a minimum.

8 *How much judgment comes into the inspector's job?*

This will depend on the product and the method of production. It should, however, always be kept as small as possible and the standards made as objective as is practicable. The ideal is that when two inspectors check a batch of products separately, they should reject exactly the same number. And that each of the two should reject the same ones. Experiments like this will show how far they are working to an objective standard rather than relying on personal opinion.

9 *What should be done when an inspector rejects a product as not up to standard?*

When an inspector rejects a product, then his job as an inspector has been completed. It is then up to the supervisory manager to decide whether the defect is impossible to rectify and the product must be scrapped; or whether reworking or repair can bring it up to standard. This decision must be made on a basis of cost. If the time involved in reworking or repair is less than the cost of the material, labour, etc. that has been put into the product up to that point, then the expense will be justified. If, however, it is going to cost more to put it right, then the product should be scrapped and loss accepted.

10 *What do we mean by Value Analysis?*

This is a method of investigating the cost of each component and production process to find out how it contributes to the value of the finished product. It is normally carried out by a team representing each function of management concerned. Rearrangements of design or production methods result in lowered unit costs without reducing the value of the product.

CHAPTER 8 | Production Planning and Control

Harking back for a moment to the country chap we mentioned on the first page, do you think he's now got any more idea of what's going on? Can he make a bit more sense of what's happening around him? We hope so, after all this study. But we could recommend a short cut in trying to understand industrial organization. This is to think of it as a set of systems.

In another book in this series (*Principles and Practice of Supervisory Management*) there was a discussion on the structure of organization. This emphasized that the supervisory manager formed a link in a chain of responsibility and authority, running from top to bottom. This is the 'line' organization, and we must never forget its importance. In addition, however, there is the 'functional' organization, with its various specialist departments. Each of these has its own staff of trained people; its own purpose and its own way of going about that purpose. Each one is, in fact, a little 'system' of its own. And it is important that each system should function efficiently within itself, achieving its purpose with the minimum of time and manpower.

We could sum up what we have been talking about so far, in terms of such systems. For example:

(1) We have dealt with a *Maintenance System* concerned with checking the mechanical efficiency of the plant and equipment. This should provide an emergency service which can be called in to deal with anything that goes wrong. It should also provide a preventive service which makes sure that things don't go wrong.

(2) We have discussed a *Work Study System* concerned with the methods on individual operations. By the use of work measurement techniques, this can work out standards of efficiency for each.

(3) We have outlined a *Wage Payment System* which negotiates the higher earnings that will be paid for increased efficiency in these operations.

(4) We have also thought about an *Inspection or Quality Control System* for checking products as they are made, to ensure that they are up to the specifications laid down by the designers.

As well as working effectively within themselves, however, these systems must fit in with the purpose of the organization as a whole.

Things go wrong when they start getting at odds with one another or when they start competing with the line organization. Little 'private empires' are not unknown in some organizations. The only way to prevent this is by all the people concerned being in one another's confidence, knowing what each is trying to contribute, and understanding one another's work.

The Study of a Production Problem

Up to now we have been concerned with the factory itself, with its layout, its capacity, the routings within it, methods of transport, and so on. But we have not yet thought about producing anything in it. This, then, is the next point we must turn to. We must consider the system by which the productive activity of the organization is planned and controlled. We must begin with a study of the operations involved in the making of the products. Only when we know how long these take, what material they require and what sequence they form, can we start any realistic plan.

To give a very simplified example of a production planning problem, let us think of a square container. It measures 6 in by 6 in across, and is 6 in high. It is made from five 6 in by 6 in plates of metal, one for the base and one each for the four sides. These are riveted together on four angle irons, and the seams are soldered. The diagram (Fig. 27) shows what the finished product looks like. (It may not appear to be of much use for anything. However, we are only going to use it as an example, not to put things in.)

The method of production is equally simple. The bottoms and sides are stamped out from sheets of metal, each measuring a yard square. The angle irons have to be drilled with six holes in each, to take the rivets. Both these processes are carried out in the machine shop. It takes 6 seconds to stamp out each piece for the bottom or side of the container, giving 10 to the standard minute. And it takes $7\frac{1}{2}$ seconds to drill the 6 holes in each angle iron, making 8 to the standard minute.

The containers are put together in the assembly shop. First the bottom and sides are riveted together on the angle irons. This takes a standard minute for each. Then the seams are soldered, which takes another standard minute.

How do you plan the production of these containers?

The first step is to work out the capacities at each stage in the process. We begin with the stamping out of the bottoms and sides. At 10 to the standard minute this gives us a production of 600 an hour. And as we need 5 for each container, one bottom and four sides, one press will provide enough for 120 containers an hour, or 960 in an 8-hour shift.

Next comes the drilling of the angle irons. Here the standard minute is 8 items, so this gives us 480 an hour. As we need four angle irons for each container, one drill will provide enough for 120 containers an hour, or 960 in an 8-hour shift.

Thus, in the machine shop, if we keep one stamping press and one drilling machine continuously at work on these parts, we shall be producing enough parts for 960 complete containers in each 8-hour shift.

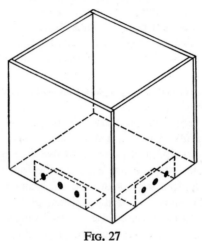

FIG. 27

Now let us look at the assembly shop. It takes a standard minute to rivet the bottom and sides on to the angle irons. Thus we should get a production of 60 an hour from this process, or 480 a shift. The same will apply to the soldering, which also takes a standard minute. Thus, if we put one operator on riveting and one on soldering, each should be able to keep the other going. Between them they should produce 480 containers a shift. But we've got parts for 960 coming through from the machine shop. That's twice as many as these two operators can deal with. So the obvious thing to do is to put four operators on in the assembly shop, two on riveting and two on soldering. These should be able to handle the output of 960 (2×480) for which parts are coming through each shift from the machine shop.

By now we've got our production process streamlined. But what about the flow of material we need to keep this going? Every day we're going to need:

> 4,800 bottoms and sides (five to each container). As we get 36 of these out of the 36 inch square sheets, this is going to mean 133·3 sheets a day. To allow for wastage in stamping, we'll call this 135 sheets.
>
> 3,840 angle irons (four to each container). Again, to allow for wastage, we'll call this 3,900.
>
> 23,040 rivets (twenty-four to a container). And as these little things get lost easily, we'll call this 24,000.

Putting the Plan into Action

This, then, is the amount of material that has to come forward every day from the stores to keep the production process going. And this little exercise should illustrate the kind of planning that has to be done if we are to make the best use of plant and personnel. It is, of course, not so simple as this in real life. Most products will be more complex and will require more parts and more work than our silly little containers. You have only to think of a motor-car to get some idea of the problems of real-life production planning. Then again, can we always rely on the production figures being exact to the estimates in the plan? Obviously not, for there are breakdowns of plant, absences of personnel, and other hold-ups to interrupt production. Someone has to do something about these, and this is where the difference between planning and putting the plan into action makes itself felt. Production planning is an intellectual exercise—a matter of working out estimates from machine capacities, time studies, and so on. It is best done off the job, where the planner can get peace to do his sums, work out his quantities and machine loadings, and relate one stage in the production process to the next. The completed plan will be the result of all these calculations and will be correct to the smallest detail. But so far, it only exists in the mind of the planner, or on the charts and lists he has prepared.

Putting this plan into action is quite another matter. This is usually the task of the supervisory manager. It involves seeing that each stage of the plan is actually carried out to the times allowed. It involves foreseeing anything that might hold up the execution of the plan. And it involves taking action to make sure that these interruptions do not, in fact, happen.

In a jobbing shop, there is less opportunity for this overall planning. Each product will be a one-off job, made to its own specification. Machines will be multi-purpose, set up and operated specially for each job by a skilled operator. It may be possible to make an estimate of the work load for the section, but this will only be in general terms. The detailed planning will remain in the hands of the supervisory manager. He is the only person who can make sure that maximum use is being made of the plant and that the operators are doing an adequate day's work.

By skilful design, however, more and more production is moving on to a flow or automation basis. And this is where the nature of the supervisory manager's job is changing. Instead of doing his own planning, making up his own work schedules, and controlling everything that goes on in the shop, he finds himself working with specialists. At the moment we are concerned with those involved in production planning and control. There are others which we have already discussed, and it is important that the supervisory manager should understand what they are all trying to do. They work out the plans or schedules, but he puts them into practice on the job. And it is on him that the results depend.

Production planning, therefore, is the systematic attempt to keep plant and personnel occupied to capacity, and to keep a continuous flow of work through the factory. It depends on the following steps:

1 An accurate knowledge of the output of which each piece of plant and each individual operator is capable. This depends on work measurement, which we dealt with in Chapter 5, supplying reliable timings and standards. Without this as a first step, accurate production planning will be difficult or impossible.

2 A programme of work which will keep plant and personnel occupied to capacity. We have already given a simplified example of this in our exercise on the production of containers. In real life, of course, this would be much more complicated. In a jobbing shop it could only be done in general terms with a wide margin of error. With batch production, it would be a matter of sorting out the orders in hand, noting the delivery dates, and trying to work out a programme which would allow for the longest runs with the minimum changeover. With flow production, it is essential to fit in each stage of the production process so that they are all working to capacity. This would involve making sure that the output from one operator or machine keeps the next one supplied with the parts he needs. The final assembly line in a motor-car factory

is perhaps the most impressive example of a flow production process. When we think of all the parts that have had to be produced in different departments and by outside suppliers as well, to keep the line running, we get some idea of the complexity of the planning process.

3 A supply of raw material will be necessary to keep this programme going. This will involve the purchasing department in placing the necessary orders and arranging delivery dates. Raw material, bought-out components, and everything else must be available in the stores as and when they are wanted. The internal transport system must carry these to where they are to be used. In some cases it will be necessary to have stores for partly finished products to provide buffer stocks at different stages. The production programme depends on a constant supply of stuff to work on. And an effective production plan must make sure that whatever is needed is there when it is required.

4 The whole production process must be kept under control. This is where that popular and respected figure, the Progress Chaser, makes his appearance. His task is to keep the programme continuously under review and to make sure that nothing holds it up. In flow production, this is simply a matter of checking on each stage of the process. In batch production it may mean rearranging the programme to meet sudden changes in demands for deliveries or other emergencies. So long as the supervisory manager understands the idea of production planning, he can collaborate intelligently with the progress chaser. In fact, the supervisor's attitude to him might be taken as a guide to his knowledge of the subject.

An efficient production control system can be a considerable advantage to a supervisory manager. It can relieve him of a lot of routine clerical work. If the production control staff are on the ball, they can take over the job of working out his production programme in detail. They can give him a time plan showing when operations should start and finish, with the various priorities. They can give him his machine and labour requirements, and if there are any changes in hours, they can give him early warning of overtime or possible redundancies. They can ensure that everything he needs—tools, drawings, material, special equipment, etc.—is there when it is wanted. They can plan economic batch sizes, costs of labour and material, both direct and indirect, and the other items on which the financial results of his section will depend. Provided all this planning is accurately done, it should take a load off his shoulders and leave him to get on with the more demanding task of putting the plan into action.

The Production Control System

We not only have to consider how the production control system affects the job of the supervisory manager; we have also to think about the working of the system itself. We shall spend a moment, therefore, on the various stages that have to be dealt with within a production control department.

1 Interpretation of the Sales Forecast

The general idea behind production planning and control is to keep the capacity of the factory occupied for the maximum possible time. This, however, will depend on the sales department, for it is they who must obtain the orders needed to do this. All the activities in a production organization are aimed at providing what the customer wants. Here again, we come up against the different types of production. In a jobbing shop, production control will be concerned with getting out a series of 'specials' for which the sales people have got orders, one at a time. When we move to flow production, planning on a longer-term basis becomes possible, and indeed necessary. The sales department may then be asked to provide a forecast for, say, the next three months. This will be wanted as a basis on which to plan production.

The production planning and control problem then becomes one of translating this forecast into units of manufacture. If the factory were producing a single item, like the little containers we discussed above, and if the sales forecast were reliable, the job would be a walkover. Production could be planned on a throughput of so many containers a day, labour and machine requirements could be calculated, and a supply of raw material ordered. Such an ideal situation doesn't happen very often, unfortunately. In the first place, the sales forecast is often no more than a 'guesstimate'' with a margin of error either way. Actual sales will vary from the forecast and may turn out to be less than were expected. Should the production plan then go ahead and pile up stock, in the hope that surplus items can be sold later? Someone up the line will have to decide on this. And if he makes a wrong decision, it may cost a lot of money! If, on the other hand, he decides to play it safe, the production plan will have to be cut down to suit. This will involve rearrangements of labour, machine time, supplies of material, and so on. When a number of lines are being produced in the same factory, similar problems will arise with each. In addition there may be complications with special orders over and above the standard stock lines, rush delivery dates, and the like. Translating the sales forecast into a workable production plan can be a first-class headache.

2 Interpretation of Design Requirements

The design department will have drawn up a specification for each product and prepared a series of drawings. These, however, will still have to be worked out in terms of manufacturing methods. And there may be problems here. A list of manufacturing operations must first be drawn up for each part and checked for practicability. There may be room for adaptation here. Then there is the question of whether certain parts or components could be bought from outside more economically than they can be made in the factory. If so, orders must be placed, and deliveries arranged. Questions of standardization will also arise—whether parts already in production could be used. These may involve modifications in design, especially in new models. You can imagine how these changes will need careful nursing through, before a design is turned into a satisfactory production job.

3 Process Planning

Once a production job has been boiled down into a series of operations these must be planned in sequence. The machines and tooling required for each, the type of labour, the loadings, the flow of parts or components—all of these must be thought out and balanced one against the other. If someone can concentrate on this away from the noise and bustle of a production department, he is likely to come up with a better plan. In large organizations, process planning is sometimes carried out in a separate section for this reason. In others, however, it forms part of the work of production planning and control.

4 Programming and Schedules

What matters most to the supervisory manager is that he should get a satisfactory programme of work for his section. And this is what all the foregoing should be leading up to. With a sales forecast and designs interpreted into process plans, we can now begin on the production programme, taking the various stages one at a time.

Fig. 28 shows the sales requirements for the next three months.

Complete list of products	Month	*February*						M
	Week ending	*1*	*8*	*15*	*22*	*29*	*7*	
	Week No.	*4*	*5*	*6*	*7*	*8*	*9*	
A			*200*				*200*	
B			*150*	*200*		*200*	*175*	*100*

Fig. 28

Completed products have to be ready for delivery on these dates in the quantities stated.

From this the factory programme can be completed, working backwards step by step. For example, 200 of product A are required by 8th February. Final assembly will take a week, so these must start in the assembly department on 1st February. The major components will take another week to get through the machine shop, so they must start there on 25th January. We can go through this process for each component, including those bought from outside. Fig. 29 shows how it can be laid out in what is called a 'Network Analysis'. This pro-

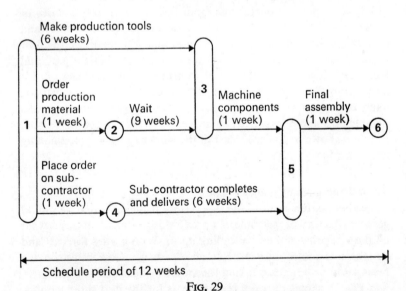

Schedule period of 12 weeks

Fig. 29

vides a means of calculating how a production plan must proceed from start to finish.

Departmental and section programmes can be taken from the

Complete list of components	Month	*FEBRUARY*			
	Week ending	*1*	*8*	*15*	*22*
	Week No.	*4*	*5*	*6*	*7*
A A	*1,000*		200 / 200 ; 200 / 200		
A B	*1,000*		200 / 198 ; 200 / 198		200 / 220 ; 400 / 418
B A	*3,000*	150 / 160 ; 150 / 160	200 / 187 ; 350 / 347	nil / 100 ; 350 / 447	200 / 100 ; 550 / 547

This figure shows the weekly scheduled requirements ·· *200* | *187* ··· This figure is the weekly deliveries

This figure is the ·· *350* | *347* ··· This figure is the cumulative weekly scheduled requirements | cumulative weekly deliveries

FIG. 30

overall factory programme. A useful means of setting these out is to show the weekly and cumulative requirements for each item. Alongside is shown the actual products made each week and also cumulatively. (See Fig. 30.)

5 Stock Control

To carry out a production programme, material and components must be available as and when they are wanted. These cost money and it is uneconomical to have large sums tied up in slow-moving stocks. What we must aim at is to keep the investment as low as possible, while at the same time avoiding the risk of holding up the programme by running short. To do this we need accurate and up-to-date records from which we can see the total stock of each item

Deliver to stores
Reorder level
Reorder quantity

Component description and No.
Product title and No.

Date	Quantity on order	Supplier	Purchase order No.	G.R.N. No.	Quantity received	Quantity out-standing	Material issue re-quisition	Quantity issued	Balance in stock

FIG. 31. *Stock record card*

at any moment. They should also show the rates of withdrawal, deliveries, quantities on order, etc. Fig. 31 shows an example of a stock record card. Depending on the type of production, there are two basic methods of stock control.

(a) *The Consumption Method.* This applies to items which are being used at a regular rate, which allows for long-term planning. From the records we should be able to calculate a Demand Rate, or the rate at which items are being withdrawn for use. Next we want a Delivery Period, or the time it will take to obtain a further supply. From these we shall be able to calculate a Re-order Level which will simply be the weekly usage multiplied by the delivery period plus a margin of error. Suppose, for example, we are using 150 units a week and it takes 4 weeks to get a delivery:

Re-order Level = Demand Rate (150 units/week) × Delivery
Period (4 weeks) + Margin of Error (600)
= 1,200

Thus if we place a new order when the stock drops to 1,200, we should be able to keep to our production programme. We have built in a margin of error (600 units or four weeks' usage) against delays in delivery or other calamities.

The Re-order Quantity will depend on things like convenient loads for transport, reduced prices for larger quantities, how often we wish to place orders, etc. This is calculated simply by multiplying the demand rate by the frequency of ordering, thus:

Re-order Quantity=Demand Rate (150 units/week) × Frequency
of Ordering (13 weeks or 4 times a year)
=1,950

Planned Minimum Stocks are simply the quantity below which it is considered inadvisable for stock to be allowed to fall. This is calculated by deciding on the number of weeks, supply to allow as a margin of error, and multiplying this by the demand rate.

Planned Minimum Stock=Demand Rate (150 units/week) × Delivery
Time (4 weeks)
=600

The Consumption Method has all the advantages of planning ahead. One of these is the opportunity of making favourable purchases when the market is going your way.

(b) *The Commitment Method.* This applies where particular quantities have to be ordered to meet specific needs. It will be the usual method in jobbing production. The problems here arise mainly over waiting for deliveries, particularly of raw materials and non-standard parts, which have to be specially made. Minor variations are:

> *Pre-commitment*, where parts or materials are ordered in advance, knowing that the customer's order will follow.
>
> *Post-commitment*, where purchases are only authorized after receipt of the customer's order.

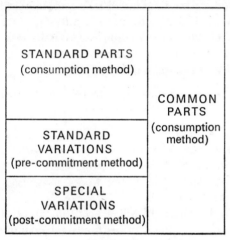

FIG. 32

In any organization, these various methods of stock control will usually be going on at the same time (Fig. 32). The Consumption Method will apply to standard parts and common parts, the Pre-commitment Method to standard variations, and the Post-commitment Method to special variations. To maintain a steady flow of production, the more common and standard parts we can use, the better. This will have enormous advantages in lower costs, steady employment, and maximum use of resources. Thus, when your wife complains that all the cars look the same, that she can't get the exact size of washing machine to fit under the sink, and she can never find the shade of colour she wants, don't try to argue. Just remember that you'd never be able to afford half these things if they were made on a one-off basis.

6 Storekeeping

This may not always come under production control, but in view of the importance of stock control, the two must work closely together. The stores should always be working ahead of the production programme, so that factory requirements can be met and lost time avoided. We have already dealt with the main essentials of stock control, so that the problems of actual storekeeping should now fall into place. They are mainly concerned with planning the use of space. And with an adequate stock control system it should be possible to calculate maximum and minimum stock levels. No item should fall below the planned minimum, so that space must always be available for this. When a delivery has been received, the re-order quantity must be added, which will represent the maximum stock which must be planned for. Stock records will be compiled from bin cards kept in the stores. It is therefore essential that these should be accurate and up to date.

7 Progress

This is the 'universal watchdog' aspect of production control. It depends on a continuous flow of information about what is happening in each section and department of the factory. The perfect supervisory manager will turn in a regular series of reports and returns to supply this. Where supervision is less than perfect, or when emergencies crop up, the progress chaser must get around himself to check up on what is going on. The general idea here is to make sure that everything is going according to plan and that the programme is being carried out exactly. If there are any discrepancies, the sooner they are brought to light the better. Advice can then be given as to how these can be sorted out, priorities can be rearranged, and solutions agreed to the problems they present. The progress chaser may never exactly be regarded as everybody's best friend, but the job he does is essential to an easy production flow. And it's better for him to risk sticking his nose in too early than to wait until a really first-class pile-up has happened.

SUMMARY

1 *How should we regard the functional or specialist departments in an Organization?*

They should be thought of as 'systems' within the organization, each with its own specialist staff, its own purpose, and its own methods. Maintenance, work study, inspection, production planning and control, should each be recapitulated in these terms. While the purpose of each functional system should be achieved economically and efficiently, it is also essential that these purposes be integrated into the overall purpose of the organization.

2 *What is the purpose of a production planning and control system?*

To keep the productive capacity in a factory utilized to its maximum. This means that there should be a continuous flow of products going through with each operator and piece of equipment fully occupied during working hours.

3 *How does the sales forecast affect production planning?*

There is no point in making products unless they can be sold. Forward planning of production is thus quite pointless unless some forecast can be made of forward sales. If this is accurate and reliable, many production planning problems will be solved. If, however, accurate sales forecasting is not possible, production plans will have to be continually modified.

4 *How is production planning affected by design?*

When the specification of a new product comes from the design department, this has been thought out mainly in terms of its acceptability to the customer. It may not have been considered in detail as a production job. This must now be dealt with, and where standard parts can be used or modifications made to facilitate operations, these must be introduced and nursed through.

5 *What do we mean by process planning?*

A careful consideration of each operation in a production process, its timing, loading, and place in the sequence. This depends on an accurate knowledge of these operations in terms of work measurement. The result should be a production plan which is efficient and economical and which makes a free and fast flow through the factory possible.

6 *What does the programming or scheduling aspect of production planning and control consist of?*

The purpose here is to lay out a detailed programme of work which will keep the factory fully occupied and for which everything necessary will be forthcoming when it is required. This programme is broken down into departments and sections, so that each manager and supervisor knows exactly how his personnel and equipment will be occupied during the next period of time.

7 *What do we mean by critical path analysis?*

This is a method of working backwards from the final result to fit all the steps into a workable time plan. If a product is to be ready by a given date, each step in the production of each component can be programmed in sequence, to be ready when required for the succeeding operation.

8 *What are the two methods of stock control?*

(a) *The Consumption Method*, where items are being used at a regular rate and forward planning is possible.

(b) *The Commitment Method*, where items are bought specially for particular jobs, either before or after a customer's order has been received.

6 *What are the key figures in stock control?*

(a) *A Demand Rate*, or a rate at which items are being withdrawn for use.

(b) *A Re-order Level*, which is Demand Rate × Delivery Period + Planned Minimum Stock.

(c) *A Re-order Quantity* = Demand Rate × Frequency of Ordering.

(d) *A Planned Minimum Stock* = Demand Rate × Delivery Time.

10 *What are the problems of storekeeping?*

Mainly the keeping of accurate records of movement of each item in and out of stock. Also the planning of space for maximum and minimum stock levels.

11 *What do we mean by 'progressing' in production control?*

Keeping a check on everything that is happening through the production process to ensure that the programme is working according to plan. Any deviations should be brought to notice as quickly as possible so that something can be done to put them right.

How long is a piece of string? Is it too long? Too short? Or just long enough? Is it shorter than a piece of rope? Or longer than a piece of thread? We can go on producing variations of this ancient question as long as we like. All we are doing of course is showing up the importance of measurement. As soon as we say that a piece of string is 12 inches long, these questions answer themselves.

The word 'statistics' just means juggling with measurements. People say, of course, that there are liars, damn' liars, and statisticians. This is perfectly true, for there are a lot of ways of presenting your measurements. And it is only common sense to choose the one that makes the best of your case and the worst of the other fellow's. When he says, 'Do you realize that the inspector's refused to pass twenty products out of your section today?', you come back with 'Yes, but that's less than one per cent of the total production.' And you probably get away with it. There's a lot to be said, therefore, for having some general ideas about the use of statistics in your job.

The sensible and honest use of statistics is an essential aid to modern management. It can cut through a lot of argument based on prejudice and personal opinion. It lets people get down to the facts of the case, compare one set of facts with another, and see the differences between them. They can also try to find out what has caused these differences by relating one set of measurements to another. Whatever suspicions some people may have about statistics, they are going to be increasingly important. And in any case, these suspicions are often based simply on ignorance.

The Collection of Data

The starting-point must always be the collection of facts. And these facts must always be in the form of measurements or figures, for this is the most accurate way of expressing them. This is why the word 'data' is always cropping up in statistics. It comes from a Latin word meaning 'to give' and is defined in the dictionary as 'facts given or admitted, from which other facts may be deduced'. This sums up the whole idea rather well. You should remember, incidentally, that it is a plural word and you should always say 'these data' or 'the data are . . .'. You'll lose marks in the management one-upmanship game if you use it as a singular word, so never say 'the data is . . .'. The singular form is 'datum'.

You can only draw sound conclusions from accurate and reliable data. Thus, the first rule in statistics is to be dead sure of your original facts. Where these are quantitative, that is when they are in the form of figures, this raises no problem. If you have an accurate record of the numbers produced, the number rejected, the hours worked, how many people are absent, and so on, there is no room for argument. But where you have to get your information from other people, it may not be so simple. Then you have to rely on questions. And

Number of employees late W/E 16 Sept '67

Wk No 3	Morning		Afternoon	
Day	Male	Female	Male	Female
Mon	6	8	1	3
Tue	3	4	-	3
Wed	-	3	-	1
Thu	2	3	2	3
Fri	-	1	-	15
Sat				

FIG. 33

while you can count up the number of 'yes' and 'no' replies, you have to be careful about what they are saying 'yes' and 'no' to.

The framing of questions for collecting statistical data is really a job for the specialist. Opinion polls, market surveys, and the like, depend on questioning large numbers of people, but we hardly need to go into this here. Problems of personal bias; the framing of questions to which simple yes/no replies can be given; making sure that respondents are competent to answer; interpreting the meaning of answers: these have all been studied in detail. If they ever crop up within an organization, specialist advice should be sought. The same thing applies to data-processing equipment, punched cards, the use of computers, and the like. We shall put all this on one side and concentrate on the simpler problems that may face the supervisory manager.

Presentation of Statistical Data

The raw facts can, of course, be quite meaningless. Only when we present our data in an understandable form will they make any

9

sense. So this is where we must think about the various ways in which figures can be arranged.

1 Tabulation

This is the simplest of the lot. It just means putting our figures in suitable columns. For example, if we'd been collecting data about time-keeping we would present them as in Fig. 33.

Number of employees late Dept B W/E 16 Sept '67

Day	Total on shop pay roll	Morning				Afternoon			
		Male		Female		Male		Female	
		No.	%	No.	%	No.	%	No.	%
Mon	150	6	4.5	8	6	1	.75	3	2.25
Tue	150	3	2.25	4	3			3	2.25
Wed	150			3	2.25			1	.75
Thu	150	2	1.5	3	2.25	2	1.5	3	2.25
Fri	150			1	.75			15	11.25
Sat									

FIG. 34

We could turn these figures into percentages as well, which would make them more meaningful still. This would show that the number of latecomers from department B wasn't all that bad, as it is a large department (Fig. 34).

2 Picturegrams

Next we can turn the figures into areas on a diagram. This often makes the data easier to understand and shows up comparisons at a glance. For example, if we had four departments in a factory with the following numbers in each:

Department A	64 people
B	100 people
C	36 people
D	25 people

we could show this in the following way:

(a) by areas (Fig. 35)
(b) as a 'Pie Chart' (Fig. 36)
(c) as a 'Bar Chart' with males and females separated (Fig. 37)

Sampling

In some situations it might be a difficult and expensive business to collect all the data—so expensive, in fact, that the results would not be worth the money. We might then decide to pick out a selection of items from the total, or to take a 'sample'. And the problem which this raises is how far we can rely on our 'sample' to give us a fair representation of the total or 'parent' population.

Statisticians have studied this problem and have come up with a Theory of Probability or a Law of Statistical Regularity. What this adds up to in our simple terms is that we can be reasonably confident that a relatively large number of items chosen at random will be almost sure to have the same characteristics as the whole group. This, however, is rather a tricky sentence. For in addition to slipping in 'almost sure' and 'reasonably confident' we have mentioned two very important points. How large is a 'relatively large' number? And how do we choose a 'random sample'?

The first of these will depend on a number of things we shall not try to go into. In most of the situations you will come across, a 10% sample is usually considered large enough. There are complications but we shall leave them to one side at the moment.

It is more important that you should get a firm grasp of the second point. A *random sample* is one chosen in such a way that every unit in the total bulk stands an equal chance of being selected. It can then be said to be free of 'bias'. Bias can arise from various causes, and one of the most common is the human element. If, for example, we were to ask a young, unmarried supervisor to choose a sample of female employees for a survey, we would run the risk of having certain physical measurements, hair colouring, and facial expressions over-represented. We must, therefore, find a way of discounting his susceptibility to feminine charms and getting the right proportion of blondes, busts, and bitches into our sample. There are various methods of cutting down bias, and while we can never be absolutely certain that our sample is completely representative, we can at least use a systematic approach.

1 The Lottery Method

If we put each of the cases in the total population on a card, mix them up and take out a sample as though they were a pack of

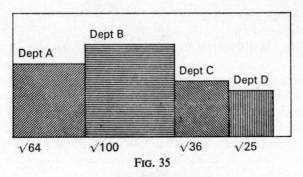

FIG. 35

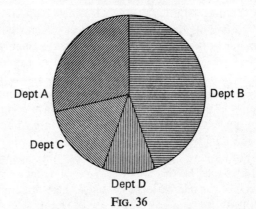

FIG. 36

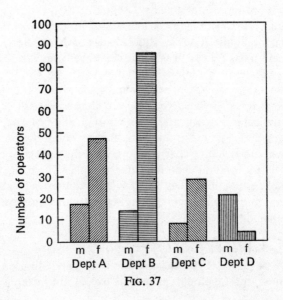

FIG. 37

playing-cards, this will eliminate the personal element. We cannot be sure, however, that the cards we have picked were really a random selection.

2 Random Number Tables

Items can be arranged and numbered in order from 1 upwards. Then we take a specially designed table of random numbers and pick

	a	b	c	d	e	f	g
1	10480	15011	01536	02011	81647	91646	69179
2	22368	46573	25595	85393	30995	89198	27982
3	24130	48360	22527	97265	76393	64809	15179
4	42167	93093	06243	61680	07856	16376	39440
5	37570	39975	81837	16656	06121	91782	60468
6	77921	06907	11008	42751	27756	53498	18602
7	99562	72905	56420	69994	98872	31016	71194
8	96301	91977	05463	07972	18872	20922	94595
9	89579	14342	63661	10281	17453	18103	57740
10	85475	36857	53342	53988	53060	59533	38867
11	28918	69578	88231	33276	70997	79936	56865
12	63553	40961	48235	03427	49626	69445	18663
13	09429	93969	52636	92737	88974	33488	36320
14	10365	61129	87529	85689	48237	52267	67689

etc.

FIG. 38. *Part sample page of table of random numbers*

out the items as they appear on the table. This goes a step further in giving each of them an equal chance. (See Fig. 38.)

3 Systematic Sampling from Lists

Items can be arranged in some sequence which arises out of the information they contain. In dealing with people, for example, we could list their names in alphabetical order. With other things, we could list them in date order or as they happened. Having decided on the size of the sample, we could express this as a percentage. If, for example, we wanted a 10% sample, we could take every 10th item on the list. There is always the possibility, however, that a source of error might have crept into our listing, such as too many of a certain type of person having names starting with the same letter of the alphabet.

4 Stratified Sampling

Another method of guarding against bias is to split up the total number of items into groups or layers. We can then use one of the above methods to take a random sample from each group. There may be a complication here if the groups differ in size. We can, however, make sure that we keep the same proportion in each group as we want in the total population. If, for example, we wanted a 10% sample of groups of 50, 30, and 20, we would take 5 from the first, 3 from the second, and 2 from the third.

As we have said, there is no magic which will make our sample absolutely reliable every time. Common-sense use of one or other of these methods, however, will go a very long way to cutting down the possibilities of error.

Graphs

It is often useful to know how one set of measures is related to another. We know, for example, that it takes time to learn a job and we don't expect a 100 performance from a chap on his first day. His output will build up as time goes on. But does it build up at a regular rate? And how long does it take him to reach 100 performance? Does every new starter take the same time? These are questions that

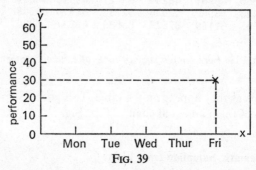

Fig. 39

might be very important when we are planning a new process. They are problems of relating two measures: time on the one hand and work-measured performance on the other. This is where a graph comes in handy.

Graphs are made with two lines or 'axes' at right angles to each other. Each line is marked off to show the measurements we are concerned with, starting at zero. Both scales of measurement start at the same point, where the two lines meet. Both are at zero here and this is known as the 'point of origin', shown by 'O'. The horizontal line, OX, known as the 'X-axis', represents one scale of measurements, in this case the number of days on the job. The vertical line OY, known as the 'Y-axis', represents the other scale, in this case performance. Thus, if on his fifth day the new starter reaches a 30 performance, we would go five days along the X-axis and thirty points up the Y-axis and put a dot on the graph.

Week		Performance	Week		Performance
1	Mon	25	5	Mon	95
	Tue	26		Tue	97
	Wed	26		Wed	98
	Thur	29		Thur	99
	Fri	30		Fri	100
2	Mon	32	6	Mon	100
	Tue	35		Tue	100
	Wed	40		Wed	98
	Thur	45		Thur	100
	Fri	52		Fri	100
3	Mon	60	7	Mon	100
	Tue	64		Tue	103
	Wed	68		Wed	105
	Thur	69		Thur	105
	Fri	70		Fri	103
4	Mon	73	8	Mon	100
	Tue	78		Tue	100
	Wed	83		Wed	98
	Thur	90		Thur	100
	Fri	95		Fri	98

FIG. 40

If this is clear so far, we can now go on to plotting his performance over a series of days. The table shows his record over his first eight weeks on the job.

These figures can be transferred to the graph in the way described above, to give a series of dots which can then be joined up by a line. We now have an accurate picture of how this new starter's performance has increased as he learns the job (Fig. 41).

But, you may say, this is only one case. This chap may have been exceptionally quick and picked up the job in remarkably short time.

Or he may have been a pretty idle type and taken far longer than he should have done. You can't say that this line on the graph gives any

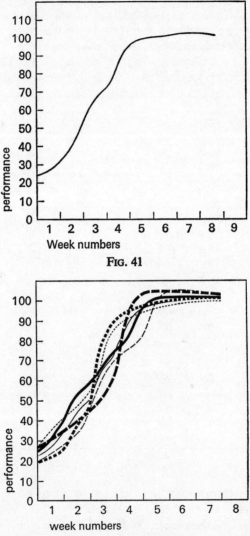

Fig. 41

Fig. 42. *Learning curve of five operators with trend line*

guide to what to expect when a lot of people are learning that job. Fair enough! But there is no reason why we shouldn't show the performance of a lot of people on the same graph. Fig. 42 shows how this can be done. And it also shows how most of the lines follow a fairly similar pattern, and how the dotted line can be used to trace this pattern.

This illustrates how a graph can be used to show 'trends'. We have already mentioned how important it is in management to have forecasts on which to base our plans. And very often these forecasts can be made from the trends shown on a graph. In this case, for example, if we were planning the output on a new process, we could expect a 50 performance from new starters after a couple of weeks on the job. We would have to wait four weeks, however, before we could rely on anything near a 100 performance.

We might draw attention to another point here. You will notice that the increase in performance does not follow a smooth line. There are flattish bits where improvement seems to be slower. These are known as the 'plateau periods' in a learning curve, and some people have tried to find out why they happen. This has led to the planning of training schemes on a systematic basis, and these have shown remarkable reductions in the time needed to learn various jobs.

The Z-Chart

Graphs are used in all kinds of ways in industry: to show the movements of sales, of production, absenteeism, and so on. One you may come across quite often is known as the 'Z-Chart'. This presents three different lots of information at the same time. If we were concerned with the output of a department, these would be:

1 The Monthly Production Figures

The total output for each month would be shown, and this line would move up and down for January, February, March, and so on.

2 The Cumulative Total

This shows first the January figures, then the total with February added, then with March added and so through to December. This line moves upwards along the graph, and shows how production is building up through the year.

3 The Moving Annual Total

For each month, this is the total of the twelve previous months. Thus, in January it would show the total back to the previous February, in February back to the previous March, and so on. The usefulness of this figure is that it shows the overall trend, without being seriously affected by month-to-month fluctuations.

10

These three different lines form a kind of 'Z' on the graph, hence the name. The table (Fig. 43) shows an example which would be useful in letting a supervisory manager know how he stands.

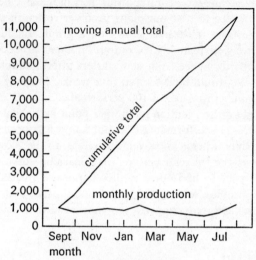

FIG. 43. *Z-chart*

Month	Output/Month	Cumulative Output	Moving Annual Total
January	1,000	1,000	9,925
February	900	1,900	10,050
March	950	2,850	10,150
April	1,000	3,850	10,375
May	970	4,820	10,200
June	1,150	5,970	10,425
July	900	6,870	9,960
August	850	7,720	9,780
September	750	8,470	9,825
October	710	9,180	9,970
November	850	10,030	10,700
December	1,250	11,280	11,280

Histograms or Block Frequency Diagrams

Graphs can be adapted to show data in the form of blocks. This is simply a matter of putting measurements on a time scale along the X-axis, and the numbers of cases in each up the Y-axis. For example, we could put a company's sales over the year into this form and show a series of blocks for each month. This is known as a 'Histogram'. (See Fig. 44.)

Suppose we use the same technique to show the variations in the size of a component. We should put the measurements along the X-axis and the number up the Y-axis in the same way. This would show the *Frequency* with which each measurement occurs in a batch.

Month	Units sold	Month	Units sold
Jan	160	Jul	250
Feb	190	Aug	275
Mar	210	Sept	290
Apr	200	Oct	325
May	315	Nov	300
Jun	330	Dec	275

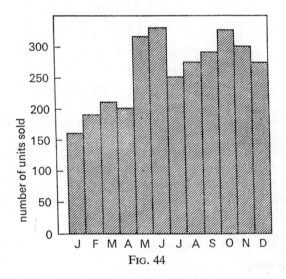

FIG. 44

When the tops of the blocks are joined up with a dotted line, this gives us a *Frequency Curve*. And when we are concerned with variations in measurements this can be very useful indeed.

Take a case where a batch of components is being machined to a certain size. If everything were going normally, we should expect most of these components to be pretty near the exact size. We should expect some to be a little bigger, getting near the upper tolerance limit. We should expect some to be a little smaller, getting near the lower tolerance limit. There would probably be a few over the upper tolerance limit, and a few below the lower. There might be the odd one well above, and the odd one well below. There is nothing mysterious about this. It is just what we would expect to happen under normal conditions.

When these measurements are plotted on a graph, the frequency curve would look like this. (See Fig. 45.)

This is known, quite naturally, as the *Normal Curve of Distribution*. It is sometimes called the Gaussian curve, after one of the men who first discovered it. It has a characteristic shape, like a bell, and simply represents the kind of distribution one would expect in

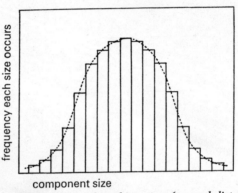

FIG. 45. *Frequency curve from histogram* (*normal distribution*)

'normal' circumstances. It is, however, a very important curve, for it can be made to reveal a great deal of information.

First of all, it can show whether the distribution is *Symmetrical*. That is, whether there are the same variations above and below the centre of the curve. This *Central Tendency* can be measured in three ways:

1 The Mode
This is the measurement with the largest number of cases in it. It will always be the highest point in the curve, so it is easy to recognize.

2 The Median
This is the middle case if they were all arranged in order from the highest to the lowest. Thus, if we had 101 cases, the median would be 51st.

3 The Mean

This is simply the average, which is worked out by adding up the total of the measurements and dividing by the number of cases. When the curve is symmetrical, all these three measures will be the

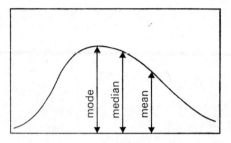

FIG. 46. *Skewed distribution*

same. When the curve is *Skewed*, however, as in Fig. **46,** these three measures will be different. The Mode will be further up (or down) the scale than the Median or the Mean. These differences can be used to calculate the amount of skewness. In checking dimensions, a 'skewed' curve will show that an abnormal proportion of components are either above or below the correct measurement. It will indicate at once the action that needs to be taken.

Variance

Another measure that can be applied to the Normal Curve of Distribution is that of Variance. Fig. 47 shows a curve which is high

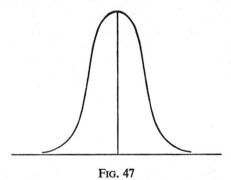

FIG. 47

and narrow, with most of the cases near the central tendency. This is a curve with only a small amount of variance, for very few cases deviate from the central tendency. Fig. 48 shows a low, widely spread curve, with more cases deviating from the central tendency. This is one with a high degree of variance. The amount can be worked out by calculating the distance of the cases from the central tendency or

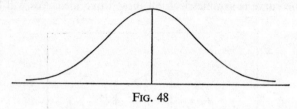

Fig. 48

mean. These can be averaged out to give an indication of how widely the curve is spread.

At this point we are getting near the border of the specialist's territory. And, as we have said, this is not a book for specialists. We shall, therefore, go on talking in simple terms, leaving out all the

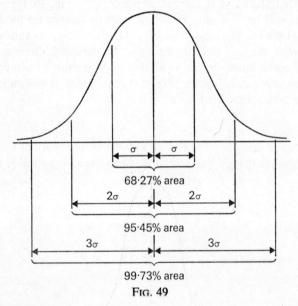

Fig. 49

detail. We shall try to explain what some of the terms mean, without going into the question of how they are calculated. If any reader wishes to follow the subject up for himself, he should try to get one of the books recommended in the reading list on page 142.

The first term to get hold of is the *Standard Deviation*. This is a measure of the variance of a normal distribution. If it is a high figure, the curve will be low and broad. If it is a low figure, the curve will be high and narrow. About 68% of the cases will fall between plus one and minus one standard deviation. About another 27%, making over 95% in all, will fall within plus and minus two standard deviations. A further 4% or so, making over 99%, will fall within plus and minus three standard deviations. (See Fig. 49.)

Quality Control Charts
These figures are helpful when we come to estimate 'Probabilities', which is a very important statistical technique. It helps to determine how far a 'sample' will be representative. If the standard deviation is small, then the chances are that a small sample will give a reliable idea of what the total number is like. If the standard

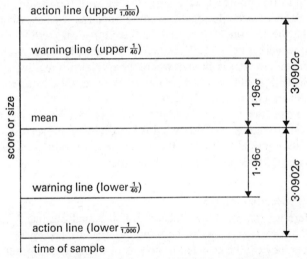

FIG. 50. *Statistical quality control chart for individuals items*

deviation is large, then there is more likelihood that a small sample will be unreliable.

Probability theory is useful in quality control. If we can assume that there is very little chance of more than 1 product in 10 being defective, then a chart can be drawn up based on a normal distribution. Each article in the sample is tested on 'Go–No-go' gauges, and the number defective plotted on a graph. Control limits are obtained from the standard deviation, and lines are drawn to indicate these. If the samples fall outside plus or minus two standard deviations, this is taken to have a 1 in 40 'significance'. This is known as the 'Warning

Line'. If they fall outside plus or minus three standard deviations, this has a 1 in 1,000 significance. The line at this level is known as the 'Action Line'. Fig. 50 shows a Statistical Quality Control Chart of this type. If more than 1 plot in 20 were to fall above or below the inner control limit, this would be evidence of lack of control. If more than 1 plot in 500 were to fall above or below the outer control limit, it would mean that the process was statistically wrong.

This explanation is, admittedly, very sketchy indeed. It is hoped, however, that it will enable the reader to recognize a Quality Control Chart when he sees one. And that he will have a general idea of what it signifies.

Records for the Supervisory Manager

Up to this point we have been dealing with the various ways in which figures can be presented. And we hope that by now the reader feels that he can understand the simpler statistical methods that he may come across at work. Things can, of course, become much more complicated, for this is an area where the specialist is making a bigger and bigger contribution. And some of the specialist's methods can become very complicated indeed.

We can turn now to the kind of records a supervisory manager will need to keep a check on what is happening in his section. These could be considered under three headings: Production records, records of Quality, and Personnel records.

1 Production Records

Here we shall first be concerned with actual output. A lot will depend, however, on what is being produced. If they are single products they can be counted in dozens or hundreds. In other cases, however, feet or yards, or pounds, hundredweights or tons may be more convenient. According to the product, the method of measurement will usually be quite obvious and it will also be traditional— that is to say, it has been in use for a long time. There is, however, likely to be a change not so far in the future. This is when we move to a decimal system.

At the moment, our methods of measurement in this country are completely haywire. We have twelve inches in a foot and three feet in a yard. We have sixteen ounces in a pound and fourteen pounds to a stone. We have two halfpennies to a penny, twelve pennies to a shilling, and twenty shillings to a pound. Thus when we buy fourteen-and-three-quarter stones at four-and-ninepence-halfpenny a pound, we have landed ourselves with a nice little sum in arithmetic. If we have to add a further cost in transport of sevenpence-halfpenny per ton-mile, it is a wonder that anyone ever pays the correct price for anything. The answer to all this nonsense, of course, is the decimal system where everything goes by tens or multiples of ten. Thus we have a hundred cents to the dollar, ten millimetres to the centimetre, a hundred centimetres to the metre, a thousand cubic centimetres in a litre, and so on. All this makes the sums much easier and it is likely that we shall soon get rid of our fourpences and furlongs and other out-of-date stupidities.

Leaving these complications aside, there should be no problems in recording the output of a section by the day, the week, or any convenient period. The question of standards may, however, arise.

Compon-ent	Capacity	Production	% production	Scrap	% efficiency
AA	1,000	950	95	50	90.4
AB	350	300	85.71	10	96.67
BA	500	400	80	5	98.75

Fig. 51

For even though a section's figures may be up on last week or last year, they may still not be as good as they might be. To deal with this point, it may be advisable to show the output figures as a percentage of actual capacity. Suppose the machines in a section are capable of producing 1,000 units a day, or 5,000 over a 5-day week. This would be the figure if they were to be kept working at full capacity every minute of the day, a figure of maximum possible output. Such a figure would be impossible to attain in normal working, of course, for there will be unavoidable stoppages for resetting and other servicing. The actual output over a period could, however, be shown as a percentage of that figure, as in Fig. 51. This would give a much more realistic picture of the performance of the section concerned.

This whole idea of rates or index figures is something you should try to get used to. Crude figures are often not very informative. In fact, they can give quite a misleading impression. It may sound horrifying to quote that there were so many accidents on the motor-ways last year. But when these are expressed as a rate per vehicle-mile, it becomes clear that motorways are about twice as safe as any other kind of road.

2 Records of Quality

Spoilt work costs money, and it is essential to keep it as low as we can. To do this we must know where we stand. And for this, records of the proportion of rejects are necessary. Here again, the manner in which these are presented will depend on the type of product. In most cases, however, percentage figures will be adequate.

3 Personnel Records

In any organization, each department or section will have an authorized number of personnel. This will be calculated in relation to the work expected of it. But there may be day-to-day variations in this 'establishment' which should be recorded. These are:

(a) *Absentees*

People will be off work for various reasons. And if, over a period, only 85% of the authorized establishment are actually at work, this figure will affect output-per-man-hour calculations. It may be advisable to break the absentee rate down according to reasons: illness, avoidable absence, and so on.

(b) *Labour Turnover*

People leave and have to be replaced, raising problems of training new starters and allowing time for them to reach piecework speed. This turnover of labour is calculated by expressing the number of leavers as a percentage of the total staff over a year.

(c) *Timekeeping, etc.*

Other figures can be worked out for the percentage of late-comers, for accidents and other happenings. These are useful in providing information about the level of effectiveness of personnel. It is always necessary to know when to stop, however, for in some cases the collection of figures seems almost to have become an end in itself.

Management by Objectives

As we said above, it is often more important to know the rate or the percentage, rather than the actual figures. Thus the number of rejects may tell us less than the proportion in each batch, and the actual output less than the percentage of total capacity. In industry we should never forget about money. For money is the most convenient and universally useful means of expressing these rates. Every single item in the working of a factory can be expressed in money terms. Floor space can be measured in so much a square foot per year; plant and equipment in so much an hour, including depreciation and maintenance; raw material in so much a ton or so much a square foot; labour in so much an hour, and so on. Everything that goes into the working of a section can be measured in pounds, shillings, and pence. And the relation of these measures to one another can be worked out.

When you are put in charge of a section, therefore, you can look at it this way. You have been entrusted with a good deal of the firm's money, in floor space, in plant, and in personnel. You can use all of this to add value to the product, by machining it, or assembling, or finishing, or whatever the section was designed to do. This added value can be calculated in the output of your section less the spoilt work. It can also be set against the floor space, plant, and labour at your disposal.

This is the general idea behind what is called Management by Objectives. And it is being used increasingly in industry as a method of measuring efficiency and, in some cases, of paying managers and supervisors. What it really does is to put a chap in charge of his own business within the company as a whole. And to relate his payment to the profitability of that little enterprise. Firms which have tried this method have been very impressed with the results. For not only does it give a sensible answer to the 'What's in it for me?' question; it makes the job a much more interesting and self-respecting one. If you decided to start off on your own and set up a garage or a shop or a little engineering works, you'd have a lot of worries and problems. But you'd also get a lot of satisfaction out of making a success of it. Management by Objectives gives the same sort of satisfaction in a large organization and lets the individual know the standards on which he's being judged.

In practice, top management will lay down the company's policy for the next period of activity. This should be clear as to objectives but will not go far into detail. From it the objectives of each of the major functions of the company should be worked out. These again can be broken down for each department and section of the organization. The target for each manager and supervisor will then emerge. In achieving these, they will be making their planned contribution to the targets of the organization as a whole.

SUMMARY

1 *What is the starting-point in any statistical project?*

The collection of accurate and reliable data. These should be expressed in measurements so that they can be handled by statistical techniques. Unless the original data can be relied on, any conclusions drawn from them will be of doubtful value.

2 *What are the methods of presenting statistical data?*

(a) *Tabulation* or putting the figures in appropriate lists or columns.
(b) *Picturegrams* or turning the figures into areas on a diagram.
(c) *Graphs*—see below.

3 *What do we mean by 'sampling'?*

When, for one reason or another, we cannot deal with all the data, we must make a selection. This selection, or 'sample', must be chosen in such a way that each item stands the same chance of being picked, and it must be large enough to be representative. 'Bias' can be cut down by using either the Lottery Method, Random Number Tables, Systematic Sampling from Lists, or Stratified Sampling.

4 *What purposes do graphs serve?*

They enable the relationship between two sets of measurements to be demonstrated. One scale is shown along the X-axis, the other along the Y-axis. Data can then be plotted against each scale of measurements and joined up by a line.

5 *What do we mean by a 'trend' on a graph?*

When a number of lines seem to follow the same overall pattern, this shows that they have a similar trend. Such trends can be illustrated by drawing in a line which follows the general pattern.

6 *What is a Z-Chart?*

This shows three sets of data on the same graph. These are:

(a) *Individual figures* on a time scale.
(b) *A Cumulative Total* on the same scale.
(c) *A Moving Annual Total* for each previous twelve-month period in succession.

7 *What is a histogram?*

A graph which shows figures in blocks of varying sizes. When the tops of these are joined, they give a Frequency Curve, showing how many cases there are in each unit of measurement.

8 *What is the normal curve of distribution?*

This is a frequency curve where most of the cases fall in the middle of the range. There are fewer cases above and below, and very few further above and below. It has a characteristic bell-shaped appearance.

9 *What do we mean by a symmetrical curve?*

This is where all the measures of the Central Tendency are the same. These are:

(a) *The Mode* or the measurement with the largest number of cases in it.

(b) *The Median* or the middle case when ranged from the highest to lowest.

(c) *The Mean* or average, which is the total of the measurements divided by the number of cases.

Where these measures differ from each other the curve is 'skewed'.

10 *What do we mean by the standard deviation?*

This is a measure of Variance. If the standard deviation is large, the curve will be low and broad. If it is small, the curve will be high and narrow. Sampling will be easier and more accurate in a curve with a small standard deviation.

11 *What is a standard quality control chart?*

This shows a line with the exact measurements required. Above and below this are Inner and Outer Control lines, worked out in terms of the standard deviation. The Inner Control line is known as the Warning Line and, on a 1 in 10 expectation of defective products, if 1 in 20 plots fall outside this line, control is slipping. The Outer Control line is known as the Action Line, and if 1 in 500 fall outside this line it means the same thing.

12 *What records does the supervisory manager need to keep control of his section?*

(a) *Production Records* of output in terms of capacity.

(b) *Records of Quality* or proportions of rejects.

(c) *Personnel Records* of absenteeism, labour turnover, timekeeping, etc.

13 *What do we mean by management by objectives?*

Figures like the above can be used to measure the efficiency of a factory or a department or section within it. Standards of expected performance can be set in terms of these figures. The supervisory manager's effectiveness can then be measured on these standards.

Further Reading

Battersby, A. *A Guide to Stock Control.* Pitman, London (1962).

Buck, C. H. *Problems of Product Design and Development.* Pergamon, Oxford (1963).

Currie, R. M. *Financial Incentives.* British Institute of Management (1963).

Currie, R. M. *Work Study* (2nd edition). Pitman, London (1963).

Grohmann, C. J. *Principles and Practice of Statistics.* Harrap, London (1964).

Lockyer, K. G. *Factory Management.* Pitman, London (1962).

Milward, G. E. (Ed). *Organization and Methods.* Macmillan, London (1959).

Motterham, J. *Projection Control.* Industrial Administration Group. University of Aston in Birmingham.

Glossary of terms in Work Study, BS 3138: 1959. British Standards Institution, London.

Index